MESOPOTAMIA

In the same series:

ANATOLIA (2 volumes)

BYZANTIUM

CELTS AND GALLO-ROMANS

CHINA

CRETE

EGYPT

THE ETRUSCANS

GREECE (2 volumes)

INDIA

INDOCHINA

INDONESIA

MEXICO

PERSIA

PERU

PREHISTORY

ROME

SYRIA–PALESTINE (2 volumes)

ARCHAEOLOGIA MVNDI

Series prepared under the direction of Jean Marcadé, Professor of Archaeology at the University of Bordeaux

JEAN-CLAUDE MARGUERON

MESOPOTAMIA

English translation by H. S. B. HARRISON

THE WORLD PUBLISHING COMPANY
CLEVELAND AND NEW YORK

CONTENTS

PREFACE

This is the first volume of a new series.

Stroke by stroke, Archaeologia Mundi *will attempt to fill in the picture of archaeological research throughout the world and to draw the portrait of a science that is still apt to be misunderstood. The general public is passionately interested in the romantic side of archaeology. On the other hand, it can be quickly bored by the jargon of specialists in this field, and their hair-splitting disputes. It is time to counter these distortions of the subject by a more realistic and accurate approach.*

Archaeology is a science. It is not, as legend would have it, a fortuitous combination of luck and imagination. Like all sciences it is a product of human curiosity and reason. It uses precise methods aimed at achieving precise results. Its real purpose is not to fill the museums with startling, lavish and unusual exhibits, nor to provide spectacular excavation sites for the admiration of tourists. By painstaking research into the fascinating problems presented by the civilizations of the past, it reaches farther and farther back into the mists of time and the very origins of the human race.

This difficult and complex science is being practised in extremely varying conditions all over the globe, from America to China, and it is obviously impossible to become an expert in any of its branches without long and arduous training. But the layman can, at least, gain an insight into the why and wherefore of archaeological research, understand its aims and meaning, and evaluate its success. Eminent scholars and acknowledged authorities in the field have agreed to present the material in „the vernacular" for the general public in the form of an original essay by each expert on his own speciality. Numerous illustrations have been assembled by the publishers according to the authors' own instructions; they will make an important contribution to the little known or unpublished documentation on the subject.

The order in which the volumes of Archaeologia Mundi *will appear has not been fixed in advance; there is no set scheme or preconceived plan. As our collaborators deliver their manuscripts and the photographic files are ready, the books are printed and distributed. There may sometimes be a rather abrupt change as we move from America to the Far East, from Prehistory to the Byzantine age, or from conventional excavations to experimental ones where* avant-garde *techniques are being tried. But all this will not matter –*

on the contrary, it will clearly illustrate the lively diversity of the changing facets of archaeology.

Nevertheless, we are fortunate in being able to begin with Mesopotamia. It provides a first class example of the way in which archaeology has advanced historical studies, both in supplying fresh written sources and in revealing unknown perspectives of the first ages of civilization; moreover, the invention of agriculture, the advent of metal and the discovery of writing are among the most stirring events in the epic of humanity. It also affords a splendid example of the progress made by archaeological methods and aims. The special stratigraphy of the Mesopotamian mounds and the many difficulties involved in clearing clay buildings have greatly contributed to more highly disciplined methods of excavation. And the importance of the discoveries in the Land of the Two Rivers have surely earned the so-called ,,auxiliary" science recognition in its own right.

CHRONOLOGY

6th mill.	Appearance of the first villages – Muallafat
5th mill.	Peopling and settlement Periods: Hassuna, Samarra, Halaf
c. 3500	Period: Obeid
c. 3200	Uruk period – birth of urban communities – writing – arrival of the Sumerians?
c. 3000	Period of Jemdet Nasr
2600–2500	Mesilim of Kish
c. 2500	First dynasty of Ur (royal tombs) Age of Lagash (stele of the vultures)
2400–2200	Period of Akkad with Sargon I Naram-Sin
c. 2200	Invasion of the Gutis
c. 2100–1950	Neo-Sumerian period Gudea of Lagash (2120) Third dynasty of Ur–destruction of Ur
1894–1595	First dynasty of Babylon
1792–1750	Hammurabi
1595	Destruction of Babylon by Mursil, King of the Hittites Kassite invasion
1155	End of the Kassite dynasty
1100	Conquest of Babylon by Teglath-Phalasar I, King of Assyria (1116–1078)
859–827	Salmanasar III
668–626	Assurbanipal
612	Capture of Nineveh by the Medes
625–539	Neo-Babylonian period
604–562	Nebuchadnezzar II
555–538	Nabonid
539	Fall of Babylon
539–330	Mesopotamia: a Perisan province
332–330	Conquest by Alexander the Great
323	Death of Alexander
323–141	Seleucid period

beginning of the first century A.D.

Spread of Christianity – disappearance of cuneiform script

A LOST CIVILIZATION REVEALED

I

Mesopotamian[1] archaeology was born at the end of March 1843, on the day when P. E. Botta, the consular agent at Mosul, brought to light a group of buildings with bas-reliefs and inscriptions on the mound of Khorsabad (Dur-Sharrukin), some nine miles north of the site of Quyundjiq (Nineveh) where he had searched fruitlessly between December 1842 and March 1843. The discovery did not go unnoticed in Paris, since a subsidy was granted to the excavator and, at his request, a collaborator was sent out from France to make drawings of the finds, some of which were rapidly deteriorating after being taken out of the ground. This was not the first attempt to make these characteristically Mesopotamian hills yield their secret. Botta had had predecessors: the Abbé de Beauchamps in 1786, and Captain Robert Mignan, an Englishman who had gone up the Tigris by boat in 1827, made some soundings; but their findings – mainly some enamelled or inscribed cylinders and bricks – were inadequate to suggest that the technique of excavation had reached a point where it could add to our knowledge of the Oriental past,

Without being a specialist, Botta was not just an ordinary amateur, and though he undoubtedly was lucky, the first discovery of Assyrian works of art was not wholly due to chance: work was being done on the East, and though few accurate data were known, the subject was not shrouded in complete ignorance.

The contribution of the Bible

The most important source available to the first research workers on the Orient was the Bible; the Old Testament gave a true picture of the history of the Chosen People, but was not used sufficiently as a historical source. It was not read to obtain information on the ancient world, but as providing material for Christian apologists. It was not until the principles of the criticism of sources and of exegesis were fully established that the Old Testament began to be regarded as a mine of historical information; nevertheless, only a limited confidence was placed in it, and while by the end of the 19th century some credence was given to biblical history from the foundation of the kingdom of David, i.e., the first millenium, there was still much hesitation about accepting the historical accuracy of the periods of Judges and the sojourn in Egypt; the history of the

Patriarchs was regarded as legend with ut any historical foundation. 20th-century historical discoveries at Ur, Mari and Uga it invalidated this way of thinking.

The Bible has to be used with a certain caution because it gives the Israelite's view of the Oriental world. The historian of Mesopotamia has to ask himself how far its accounts can add to the knowledge of his field; moreover, the picture given of the Orient by the Old Testament, rich and truthful though it may be, is incomplete. For while the Scriptures deal with all the protagonists of the international scene of their day – the Egyptians, the Neo-Babylonians, the Medes and the Persians – they do so invariably in their relation to the Chosen People; nor is the narrator or chronicler concerned so much with historic fact as with the interpretation of events. For the Scriptures relate God's great plan for his People, and it was the sacred task of the writer to explain its meaning, that is to analyse the working of God's will. This idea implies a selection of facts and their presentation in a special light. While the Bible may be regarded as a mirror of the Near East, it does not give a complete view, for each of the Oriental peoples appeared only episodically when a temporary relation existed between it and the people of Israel. It is also a fact that in the 20th century interest was focused not so much on the patriarchal period – apart from a few episodes, such as the building of the Tower of Babel – as on the Assyrian, Babylonian and Persian empires. The first archaeological discoveries concerned the Assyrian period which was known through the Bible; this coincidence was not due to chance. From then on, Mesopotamian archaeology moved methodically from the known to the unknown.

The Graeco-Roman tradition

Graeco-Latin sources also contributed to knowledge of the ancient Orient. First of all, there were acounts of journeys: from Herodotus (mid-5th century B.C.) and Xenophon (c. 427—355 B.C.) to the Roman historian Ammianus Marcellinus, a whole series of accounts of the country, the old towns and legends were available. On the basis of earlier documents – sometimes from mere legends or stories – a number of histories were compiled, many of which are known only through later writings; thus passages of the *History of Assyria and Persia*, compiled about the 5th century B.C. by the Cnidian physician Ctesias, have come down to us through the intermediary of

Diodorus Siculus. Ctesias was living at the Persian court at the very time when Xenophon was travelling through Asia Minor and the upper country of the Tigris and Euphrates with the Greek mercenaries. Thanks to *The Jewish War* and *The Jewish Antiquities* by the Jewish historian Josephus (1st century A.D.), and to the *History of the Chaldeans, Assyrians and Persians* by Eusebius, the bishop of Caesarea, we know certain features of the three *Babyloniaca* by Berosus, a Babylonian priest of Marduk (4th–3rd century B.C.). To these sources must finally be added the geographies which were more than simple accounts of journeys: the most important ones were Strabo's *Geography* (*c.* 64 B.C. to 19 A.D.) and Ptolemy's geographic descriptions of Mesopotamia dating from the 2nd century A.D.

However, the Graeco-Romans were more interested in anecdotes, marvels and legends than in a factual knowledge of the Mesopotamian world. Descriptions of Babylon, reminiscences of legends concerning Semiramis and the famous hanging gardens, a list of more or less mythical kings: that is about the sum of the Graeco-Roman contribution. The Greeks and Romans often had the same attitude towards the Mesopotamians as towards the Egyptians, the mere spectacle of the exotic being enough to satisfy their curiosity. This attitude, although a little disappointing, can partly be explained by the fact that the classical peoples were not in the habit of thinking „barbarians" worthy of much interest, except in minor matters.

Also, the Greeks and later the Romans came in contact only with a moribund Mesopotamian civilization; whether we consider that the end came with the fall of Babylon before Cyrus in 539, the conquest of the Persian empire by Alexander (334–323) or the spread of Christianity, they knew only the Persian phase of Oriental civilization when the Mesopotamian tradition had already become fossilized and incapable of renewal. However brilliant the Neo-Babylonian empire may have been, its art shows a return to ancient sources without any original creativeness, and it succumbed almost unresistingly before the Persian onslaught. This new empire, which came into being in some thirty years, was influenced by Mesopotamian civilization to which it owed in particular its script. But its late arrival on the Eastern scene and its origins prevented it from becoming completely integrated into that scene without itself deeply modifying it; thus the centre of gravity in the new empire lay much farther to the east.

The Greeks and Romans thus saw little of the real Mesopotamia: but the West grew up on the classics as much as on the Bible. Many travellers visited the East, taking with them the memory of the descriptions by Herodotus if not the actual texts; as late as the 19th century the maps of ancient Mesopotamia were drawn on the basis of information supplied by Ptolemy, despite its late date. Nothing can better illustrate the importance of this tradition.

Latter-day travellers

At the beginning of the 19th century, besides the Bible and the Graeco-Latin authors, the accounts of later Western travellers made a – mostly rather thin – contribution to knowledge of Mesopotamia. These travellers tried to identify the sites more or less by a lucky guess, though in some cases they showed really remarkable intuition; thus the first traveller known to us, Benjamin of Tudela, during his thirteen years' travels (1160–1173) from Spain to Persia in search of Jewish communities, could identify Nineveh, in 1165, with a group of hills near Mosul; he deserves great credit for this for, even with the help of local legends and toponymy[2], he could not have seen a single building to support his conclusion. The account of Benjamin's journey was not published until the 16th century when the East began to attract other travellers.

In the 17th century a new phase began with the Roman Pietro della Valle who returned from a twelve years' journey (1614–1626) bringing back from Mesopotamia inscribed bricks which he had picked up mainly on the sites of Babylon and of Muqayyar (Ur), as well as inscriptions from Persepolis which he had copied. For the first time – and this is important – material remains of the Mesopotamian civilization arrived in Europe and were available to research workers. In fact, in the 18th century interest grew in these remains of a lost script; while the deciphering of Phoenician and Aramaic by Abbé Barthélémy laid down the lines to be followed, new documents were added to the old ones: inscriptions from Persepolis brought back by the Danish mathematician Niebuhr, the kudurruz[3] or *caillou de Michaux* named after its discoverer and the *inscription of the East India House* which is a text by Nebuchadnezzar. For a long time these first finds remained an enigma; the most fanciful interpretations and translations were published, but nevertheless the initial impetus had been given. Imperceptibly and almost unnoticed, Assyriology was being born.

16

2

3

9

11

12

13

15

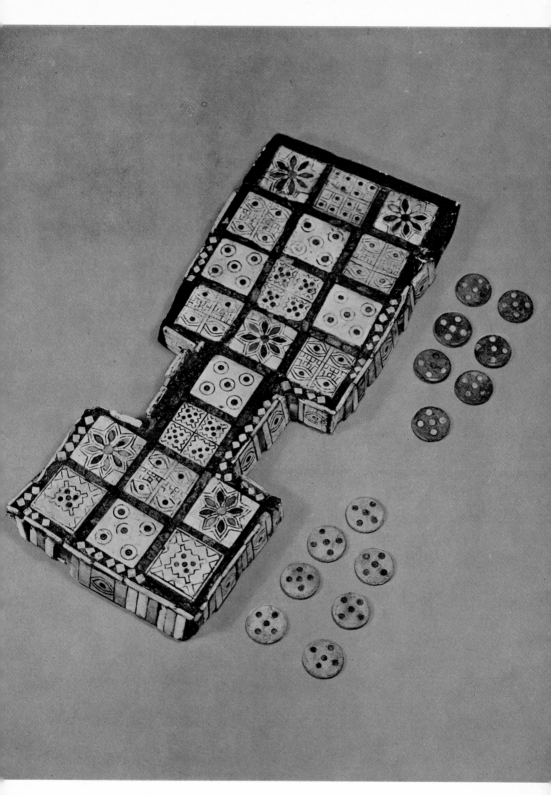

23

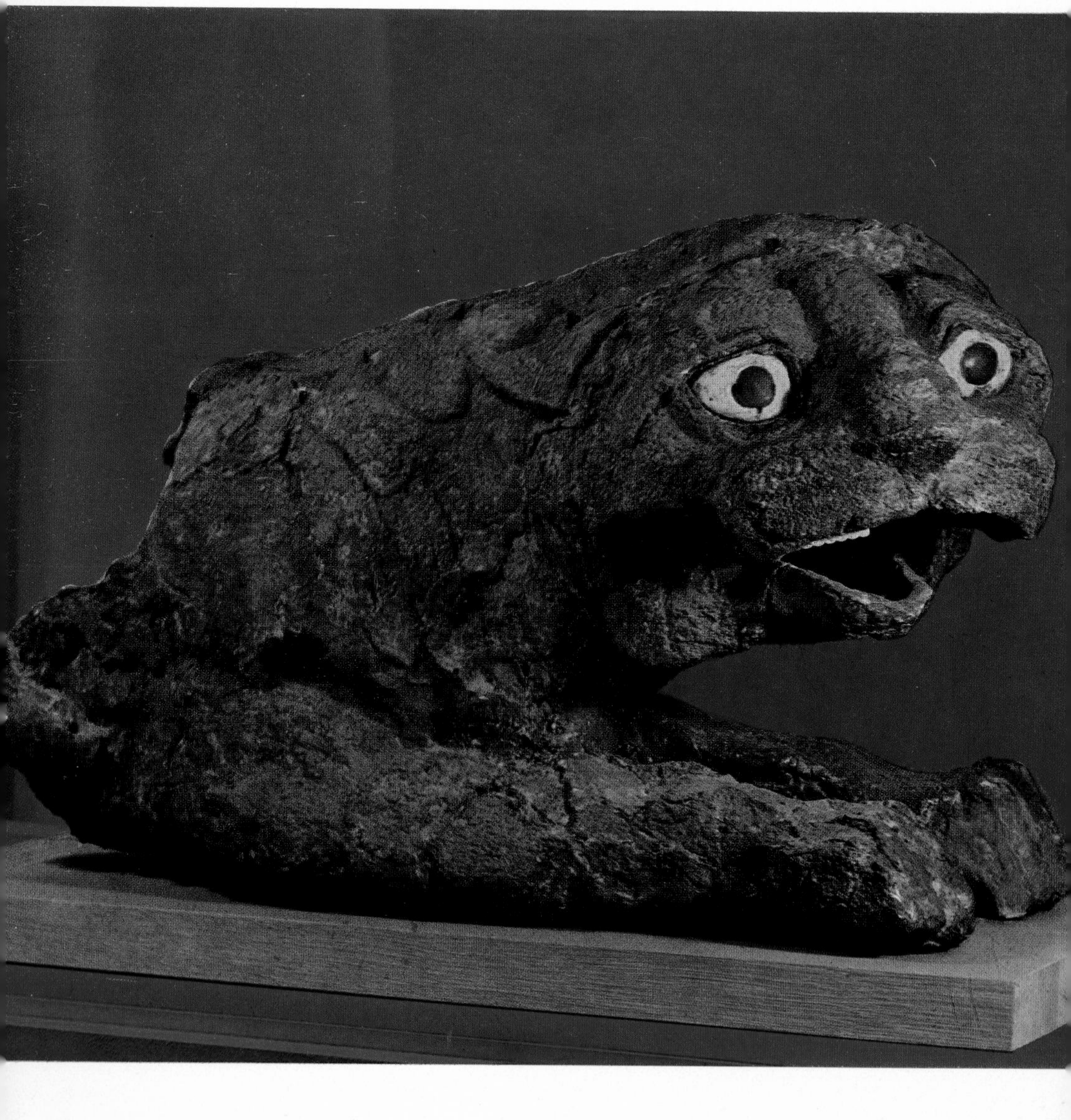

DISCOVERIES IN THE 19TH CENTURY

II

At the beginning of the 19th century a new intellectual outlook was taking shape in Europe. Influenced by the vast Romantic movement, enlightened opinion took a greater interest in the study of the past. The taste for nostalgic and solitary reveries amidst ruins turned into a wish to uncover their history, and historical studies developed considerably: the study of the national past, the deciphering of hieroglyphics by J.-F. Champollion (1822), and the initiation of prehistoric studies by Boucher de Perthes (1838) were some aspects of this new trend. However, intellectual curiosity was not the sole cause, and economic considerations also played a part in the growth of Assyriology. Napoleon's expedition to Egypt had roused British anxieties about safeguarding the route to India, and a better knowledge of land routes became necessary; there was also a great increase in the number of expeditions by British explorers throughout the East. Assyriology benefited from all these circumstances.

Assyria to the fore

Despite the vastness of the task, scholars concentrated on the small number of documents known in Europe. Since they did not – like J.-F. Champollion – have the help of the Rosetta Stone, but only a trilingual cuneiform inscription brought back from Persepolis by Niebuhr, it is astonishing that they succeeded in making out the sense of each of the three texts. A series of deductive flashes provided the basis for deciphering; once the hypotheses had been admitted that, on the one hand, the central text of the inscription was in Persian, because its position gave it pre-eminence over the other two, and that, secondly, the script was an alphabetic one, other discoveries followed swiftly. In the years preceding the first Mesopotamian excavation, a first result was achieved in two different and practically independent ways: Grotefend (by identifying a group of symbols that recurred several times as being the Persian royal title), Burnouf and Lassen reconstructed the Persian alphabet letter by letter, while Rawlinson succeeded in 1838 in reading and translating the Darius inscription on the rock of Behistun without any knowledge of the results obtained by scholars in Europe. While this did not yet amount to a knowledge of Assyro-Babylonian, it was an important step in that direction.

The important early finds of Mesopotamian archaeology roused genuine enthusiasm among the educated public to whom they "revealed", as A. Parrot said, the Assyrian world. There is a wealth of difference between the mere mention of Nineveh in the Bible and the actual exploration of the town, between biblical descriptions of the might of the kings and the experience of discovering their palaces, between ideas of the empire's size and the geographical facts. In many respects the new discoveries did not contradict the little that was known of Nineveh's power, but the Assyrian world took on a new depth, an unexpected dimension.

For forty years interest was centred almost exclusively on Assyria. During this first phase of archaeological research in Mesopotamia there were two distinct periods of activity separated by a long lull. From 1843 to 1855 the Frenchmen P. E. Botta, V. Place, F. Fresnel and J. Oppert, and the Englishmen A. H. Layard, H. Rawlinson, H. Rassam and W. K. Loftus were active, and once Botta's discoveries became known attention was directed mainly to the Assyrian triangle: Khorsabad (Dur-Sharrukin), Quyundjik (Nineveh), Nimrud (Kalakh), and Qalaat-Shergat (Assur). After an interruption of eighteen years, investigations were resumed from 1873 to 1882 by G. Smith and by H. Rassam whose zeal was directed not only to the earlier sites but also to a series of new ones, including Abu-Habba (Sippar) – an illustration of the wide range of his research. After 1882 other regions of Mesopotamia began to attract attention: Rassam himself, however, returned to England and stopped excavating. The first page in Mesopotamian archaeology had thus been turned.

During the exploration of these sites, the deciphering of cuneiform script made great progress. It is true – and this in no way detracts from the credit due to the first Assyriologists, especially as they themselves often worked also on old Persian and Assyrian – that deciphering was somewhat facilitated by the fact that the general sense of the inscriptions was now known and could be used as a basis for their interpretation; but it still remained to master the essential differences between the texts and to understand that a syllabic system, not an alphabetic one, had been used. This was shown by E. Hincks in 1846; he then assigned a number of symbols with their meaning by comparing the proper names with those in Persian texts. Rawlinson also fixed the meaning of a number of symbols and in 1851 he published the Assyro-Babylonian text of the Behistun inscription with the translation of the first column and a table of 246 symbols. At the same time excavations were yielding a considerable quantity of tablets, thanks especially to the discovery of the library in the Palace of Assurbanipal at Nineveh. From then on it was possible to intensify research: the great Assyriologist J. Oppert determined the nature, origins and peculiarities of Assyrian. However, there were many – including famous scholars – who doubted the value of epigraphic discoveries regarding that language. Admittedly, a great number of false interpretations had been suggested, including one by Count A. de Gobineau, the famous author of the *Treatise on the Inequality of Human Races*; he proposed a highly complicated system of reading and classifying 650 symbols, discounting syllabism; he asserted that the language of the tablets was Arabic, and that all the texts formed a more or less complete whole, an invocation of God which, being read backwards, became a curse. This would be no more than an amusing anecdote if it did not show the kind of thing Assyriologists were up against when trying to gain acceptance for their own discoveries which might seem quite as fanciful to the layman. To convince the incredulous of the value of the new science an experiment was organized, using the text of Tiglath Pileser I (1116–1078) which had just been discovered by Rassam; W. H. Fox Talbot sent a translation under sealed cover to the London Asiatic Society and this was not to be opened until a translation of the same text by Rawlinson had been received. To give greater weight to this experiment, the Society asked Hincks and Oppert to take part. The agreement of the different translations showed, without any remaining doubt, that the system of deciphering was valid. But fresh problems arose. Oppert had, with remarkable skill, discovered the principle of the polyphony of the symbol and the various characteristics of the language: having established its Semitic nature, he sparked off the first great controversy in Assyriology, for E. Renan refused to consider Assyrian a Semitic language. It was not until 1872 that it was admitted unanimously that Assyrian was a new branch of the Semitic family. Scholars then tried to establish the origin of this type of script and thereby sparked off the second great battle. The astonishing achievements of this forty-year period call for admiration. Not only had a new language, in a hitherto unknown script, been read and understood, but so much material was discovered and brought back to European museums that we could not possibly give even a brief summary of the items here. Despite the inexperience of the excavators and the uncertain orientation of research, the whole of the Assyrian world reappeared through its buildings and works of art: whole palaces, ziggurats, temples, hundreds of feet of bas-reliefs, monumental winged guardian bulls with men's heads, steles, kudurrus, statues, the decorations of whole buildings, tens of thousands of tablets, inscribed prisms and the famous bronze plaques covering the gates of Balawat.

At the beginning, in the first flush of discovery, no problems were raised; but subsequently false identifications and over-hasty explanations had to be corrected. Thus the excavations carried out between 1928 and 1935 by the Oriental Institute of Chicago at Khorsabad modified some of the interpretations offered by V. Place. Nevertheless, his work was considerable and formed the basis of all knowledge of Assyrian monumental architecture for a whole generation; forty years later, G. Perrot and Ch. Chipiez in their *History of Art in Antiquity* were still repeating his conclusions.

The public showed particular interest in all these discoveries, in the unloading of the cases containing antiquities and the opening of the Assyrian room in the Louvre in 1847, because everything was related to the past of a country mentioned in the Bible The biblical connection, too, was responsible for the resumption of excavations in 1872. In that year, G. Smith, a young Assyriologist who was working at the British Museum, discovered an incomplete tablet giving the Babylonian version of the Flood; this revelation had such a tremendous effect on the public that the *Daily Telegraph* offered Smith the money he needed to go to the site of Nineveh and search for the missing parts of the tablet. It was a chancy undertaking, yet Smith found another fragmentary tablet which partly completed that in the British Museum.

Taken together these discoveries revealed the warlike character, the type of language, the artistic themes and the extent of Assyrian civilization, but they offered no explanation of its origin.

The rebirth of Sumer

Unlike Assyria, Sumer was completely unknown until its existence was suggested and then proved both by philology and archaeology; in no other case, perhaps, has the complementary nature of these two disciplines been illustrated more clearly, for the rediscovery of Sumer was the outcome of both lines of research.

The slow resurrection of the Sumerian civilization did not begin until long after excavations in the East had been started. It was not, however, by chance that archaeologists were led to study first Assyria and then Sumer; soundings had been taken on all the largest Sumerian sites as if their wealth had been guessed at, but it was not yet possible to understand the things that were brought to light. It would be no exaggeration to say that the Sumerian civilization could not be recognized because the knowledge required for seeing and understanding it had not yet been acquired.

Although some travellers had ventured into lower Mesopotamia they were few in number because the country was most unattractive. The aggressiveness of certain xenophobic tribes and the extreme climate put off many travellers and archaeologists; but that alone does not explain the delay in its exploration. In fact, shortly after the discovery of Assyria, an interest in lower Mesopotamia had also been aroused; an Englishman, Sir Henry Layard (1817–1894) had lingered at Niffer (Nippur) while prospecting in 1850 and had begun research on the site which seemed most promising to him, but he did not realize that he would have to search at a greater depth than at Nineveh and, accustomed to easy successes, he soon gave up. Sir William Loftus probed Warka and Senkerah, and J. L. Taylor identified Tell Muqayyar as the town of Ur, mentioned in the Bible as being the land of Abraham; but none of them could appreciate the antiquity of the objects found, and they seemed rather poor to excavators who had been spoilt by the wealth of the Assyrian mounds. There is no better example of the bankruptcy of the type of archaeology that consists in seeking for objects without having first formed a working hypothesis and that wants at all costs to "strike it rich" rather than proceed scientifically.

Before the results of the excavation could be correctly interpreted, some epigraphists were examining problems that would give a new direction to the work. But here again it was only very slowly and item by item that conclusions could be reached.

In 1850, Hincks was the first to point out that the Assyrians had a Semitic language, but that the system of transcription by syllable went against the very nature of the language.

It seemed surprising that the Assyrians should have created such an impractical script; it seemed more likely that they had borrowed the script from another nation and adapted it to their language by dividing the latter into syllables. From then on, the nature of the problem was clear: it only remained to find the inventors of the script. A new element appeared with the discovery of syllabaries[4] and dictionaries in the library of Nineveh; this was a decisive factor in proving that another language was involved. J. Oppert studied these syllabaries and in 1859, in the *Scientific Expedition to Mesopotamia*, he thus explained the mechanism that led to the complexity of the Assyrian system: "When the Semites received the symbol meaning the head, they accepted at the same time the sound SAG which meant head to the latter (the Sumerians); but they added the sound RISH which meant head in Assyrian."[5] Another line of argument suggested to him that the origin of the people who had invented the script should be sought outside Mesopotamia: he noticed that the lion, although a common animal in the Orient, had not been given a special symbol but had been transcribed by the group UR-MAH, meaning "large dog"; thus the Sumerians came from a country where lions did not exist. The hypothesis of the extraneous origin of the people was probable, but the people itself had to be defined. In fact, the problem was twofold: on the one hand, it was necessary to name and describe this people, and on the other hand to establish its true origin. In 1855, Rawlinson had suggested Akkad, but in 1869 Oppert for the first time suggested Sumer because of ancient inscriptions mentioning "so-and-so, King of Sumer and Akkad"; he identified the Sumerians with the Turanians (a rather vague and un-scientific term, in fact, as Renan has pointed out) and the Akkadians with the Semites. In view of the Assyrian ideogram indicating Sumer and meaning language of worship, he identified Sumer as the country of the sacred language.

It is an astonishing fact that during this whole phase very methodical research was undertaken without any real controversy on the subject and the non-Semitic origin of the script was quickly admitted. But this peace was shattered with the entry on the scene of the Semitist J. Halévy with his *Critical Observations on the so-called Turanians of Babylonia* (1874), which sparked off the second great battle of Assyriology by contesting the non-Semitic origin of the script. At first he asserted that the Sumerian texts were only an ideographic edition to be read in Assyrian and that Babylonia had known only

Semitic peoples. In 1885, in reply to objections, he transformed his theory into that of ideophonics: "Contrary to the demotic system (Assyrian) which expresses words in conformity with their real pronunciation, the hieratic system (the Sumerian of the Assyriologists) shows them artificially, either by ideograms or phonograms or by a combination of the two."[6] For over twenty-five years, Halévy – who had found some supporters – and the German F. Delitzsch carried on the battle which "to him may have been a veritable holy war"[7], for he would not admit that there were people other than the Semites, that is the Jews, who could have been initiators of Western Christian civilization. This long drawn-out controversy delayed the moment when the public could accept the existence of the Sumerians. In fact, in his handbook (1904) Fossey still felt compelled to refute Halévy's theory point by point; moreover, the *Larousse Pour Tous* in two volumes which appeared in 1907, states: "Sumerians or Sumers; synonym of Akkads; name given to one of the original peoples of Lower Chaldea"; this vagueness reveals the prevailing uncertainty, particularly as almost half a column is devoted to Assyria! Nevertheless, in 1905 F. Thureau-Dangin published the *Inscriptions of Sumer and Accad* which shows how much was in fact known of Sumerian at that time.

Only Halévy's tenacity could prolong this uncertainty, for archaeology had already confirmed the findings of philology. The credit for this must be given to the French Vice-Consul at Bassorah, E. de Sarzec; having heard that there were diorite statues with inscriptions at Tello, and remembering that Taylor had prospected the region and that J. Oppert had pointed out its importance, he visited it and then started excavating, since his duties left him a certain amount of leisure. He continued to excavate until 1900. He had the perspicacity to suggest, on first seeing a large fragment of a diorite statue, that its great difference from the Oriental works of art known hitherto could be accounted for only by a difference in civilizations. His success was assured by two fortunate circumstances: thanks to inscribed statues he was able to identify the site with the town of Lagash; moreover, the mound was not covered with buildings of a later period, and from the start of the excavation Sarzec was right in the Neo-Sumerian period, so that – unlike his predecessors – he did not become discouraged. Aided by L. Heuzey, he conducted four expeditions and in 1881 the importance of his discoveries was revealed in a communication to the Academy of Inscriptions. Following this news, and while

Sarzec continued his excavation, other sites were investigated to obtain further material on this new civilization. Koldewey, a German who was later to distinguish himself at Babylon, excavated two mounds some twelve miles east of Tello in 1886, Surghul and El Hibba, which brought to light strange burial practices. The site of Niffer, which Oppert had been able to identify with the ancient Nippur and which had interested Layard, was chosen for an American expedition. In 1894 Father Scheil was working at Abu Habba (Sippar). This was the start of a more thorough research into the country of Sumer and it posed fresh problems for archaeologists.

As with Assyria, some facts were interpreted wrongly or carelessly and this necessitated later reappraisal. There was, for instance, the mistake made by Koldewey at Surghul and El Hibba: struck by the size of the tombs and their furnishings, by the partial cremation, the presence of funerary urns and the unusually narrow streets which seemed to exclude normal traffic, he thought he was dealing with veritable necropoles built with streets and houses solely for the dead. This view was not confirmed by other discoveries; it must therefore be abandoned, although some features have not yet been fully explained. Another first impression that had to be rectified was the view that the patesi[8] of Lagash whose statues Sarzec had found and to which he accorded a pre-eminent position in Sumerian art, dated back to the art of earliest antiquity in the period of Gudea; without deprecating the outstanding gifts of the Lagash artists, it must be admitted that their predecessors would have had no cause to envy their rivals of the neo-Sumerian period, as later excavations would show.

At the beginning of the 20th century scholars – with few exceptions – were convinced of the existence of the Sumerians. Nevertheless, contemporary archaeology is still preoccupied with them, as is shown by the publication in 1932 of a work by H. Frankfort, called *Archaeology and the Sumerian Problem*; there still is a problem, but it is a different one. Attempts are now being made to discover their origin, for this will lead to the discovery of the whole of Mesopotamian protohistory.

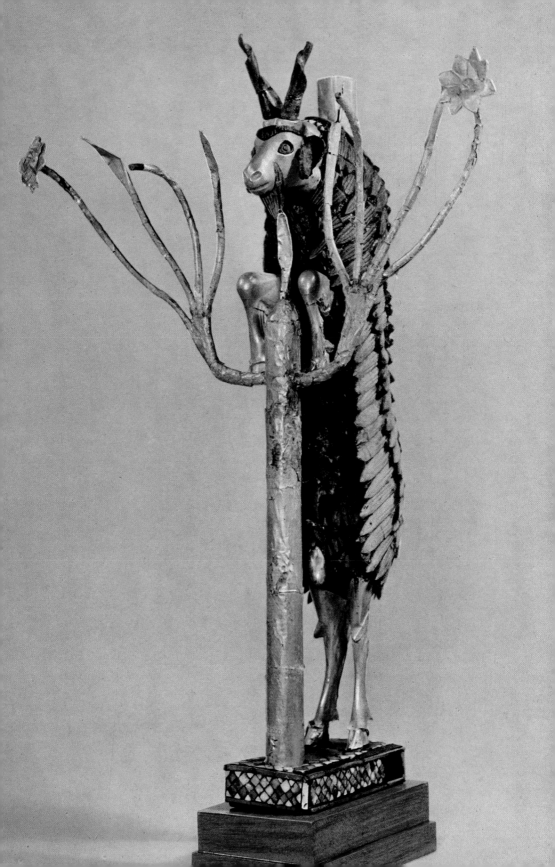

27a

27b

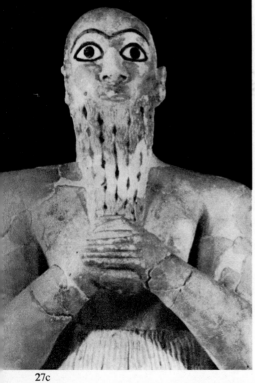

27c

27d

28

34

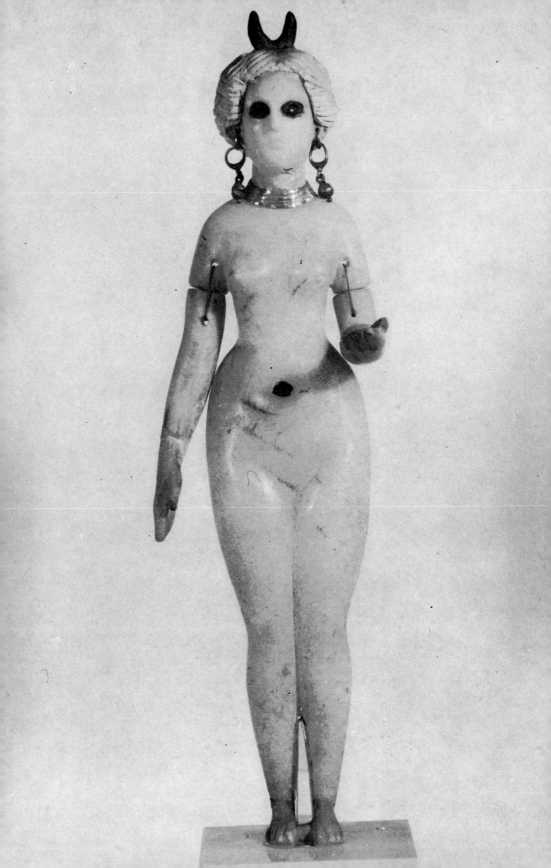

43

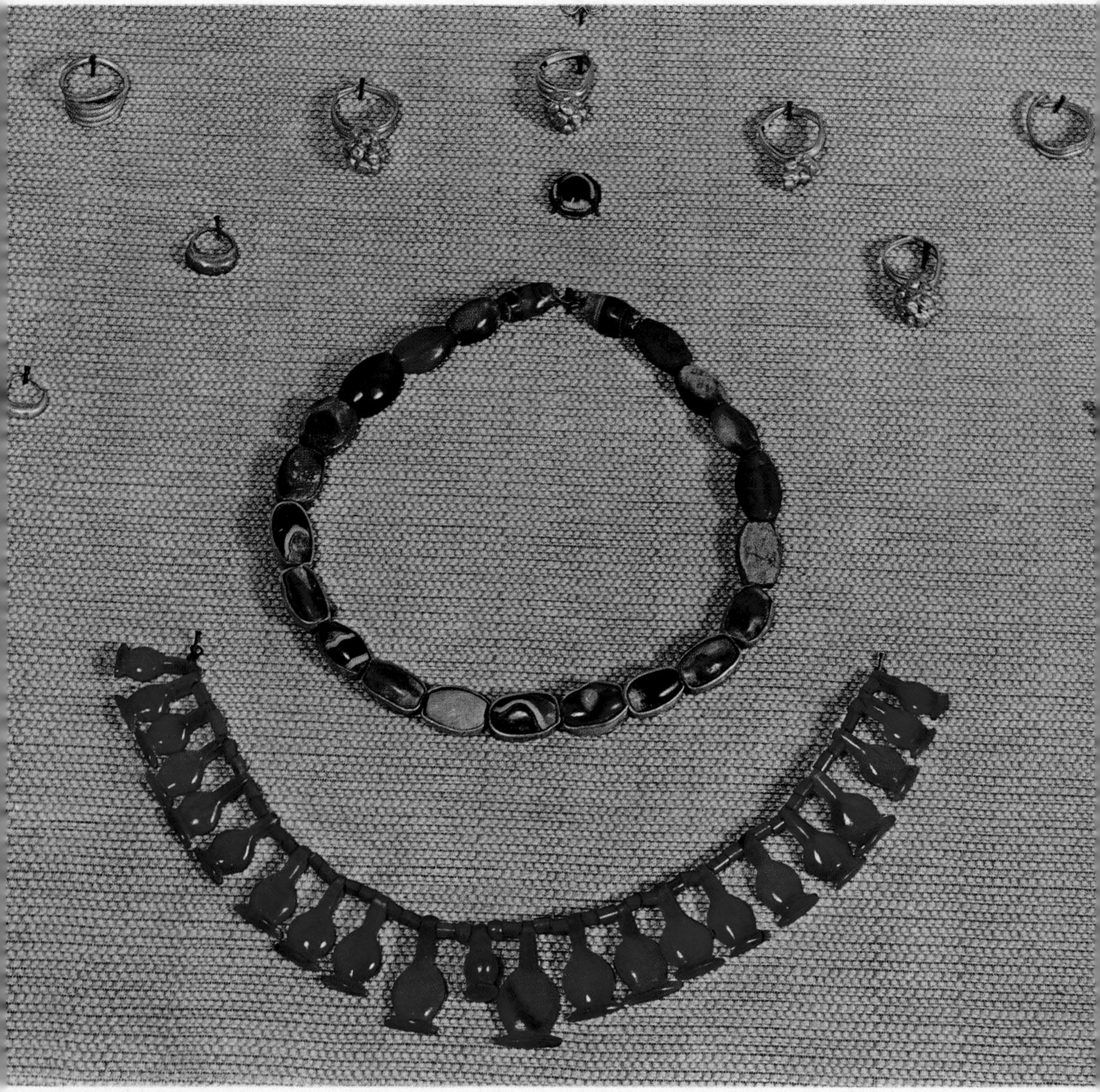

ARCHAEOLOGICAL THOUGHT IN THE 20TH CENTURY

III

Work in the 20th century has steadily aimed at extending and clarifying the knowledge gained in the 19th. The wonder aroused by the rediscovery of the Assyrian, Babylonian and Sumerian worlds led at the outset to excessive simplification; when the first discoveries had been assimilated and this fault had become evident – and since the number of objects brought to light by archaeologists was constantly increasing – it was realized that only some points could be considered as settled and that new and unknown factors were appearing. Only methodical prospecting could ensure a proper classification of the discoveries and a better approach to the truth; thanks to a surer technique of excavation and a more precise interpretation of the data through stratigraphic and chronological countersections, information has been clarified and a proper direction given to research.

Protohistory and origin of the Sumerians

"Thirty years ago it would have been impossible to write a chapter on Mesopotamian 'protohistory' ".[9] 20th-century archaeologists have tried to grasp the earliest phases of human evolution on Mesopotamian soil, and their research has been successful. Nevertheless, the first relevant finds date from the beginnings of archaeological exploration: in fact, in 1854 when Taylor was prospecting for Abu Shahrain and identifying it with Eridu, he pointed out the presence of painted potsherds. This phenomenon was rare enough to be noticed, but no further attention was paid to it; it took a longer familiarity with the items yielded by excavation to realize how very unusual painted potsherds were in a country where for 24 centuries pottery without coloured decorations had been used. The excavations of 1911 at Tell Halaf, then those at Samarra which unexpectedly yielded polychrome pottery, showed archaeologists the right path. Between the wars, a number of links were found and during the Second World War an essential age of Mesopotamian protohistory was explored on the Hassuna site. Since then, the sites of Jarmo (visited in 1945, explored since 1948) and of Muallafat (1955) have enabled research to be carried further back into the Neolithic Age, while that of Shanidar has established the juncture with the Paleolithic. It has thus become possible to study the first revolution represented by the Neolithic Age, with the aid of fresh material. While its main phases are now known, many features still remain obscure. Meanwhile, in the geographic field, well-differentiated stages of this protohistory have been fixed, although not always inventoried very accurately, on many sites both in north and south Mesopotamia. This has made it possible to compare and differentiate: it is clear that developments in the north and south do not correspond precisely. Besides the northern sites, Hassuna, Tell Halaf and Samarra, the three most important were Tell Obeid, Warka (Uruk) and Jemdet-Nasr, all in the lower part of the country; to these we must add Eridu, the holy town, doubtlessly the oldest of the Sumerian cities.

While the material available for these periods is more limited than that for the classical eras, it nevertheless offers a wealth of possibilities. It comprises, first of all, pottery, which has been particularly helpful in classifying the various periods more precisely; the different types of pottery, the decorative method of the incision, the decorative and symbolic subjects (bucranes, Maltese crosses, dishevelled women, animal friezes), the geometric or naturalist designs are all elements of comparison that make dating possible. The evolution of architecture is also of great interest: it starts modestly, in the earliest phases of Hassuna, in the shape of a small house, to culminate with the splendid – indeed, unequalled – temples at Uruk. The various tools are at first of bone, stone and clay, then of metal. The manufacture of the first seals and cylinders and the first traces of writing complete the available material whose study has – together with stratigraphic comparisons – shown sequences and breaks which give a revealing picture of continuous periods and times of abrupt change. The identification of these features has greatly exercised archaeologists, who hope they will yield a clue to the origin of the Sumerians. The scientific world has not accepted the conclusions thus obtained without some difficulty; as late as 1939, a scholar such as G. Contenau (*L'Epopée de Gilgamesh*) preferred the assumption that Sumerian civilization could be identified with that of the indigenous Asiatic background. But the variations found in pre- and protohistoric sites support the theory of major changes; it would seem strange, to say the least of it, that the Sumerians should have gone through the considerable upheavals that took place during the three millenia preceding the appearance of their script without being affected by them. There are other reasons for supporting the hypothesis of their extraneous origin: the use of stone for vases and statues and the construction of temples on terraces suggest that they came originally from a hilly or mountainous country. But archaeologists differ widely and violently as to the time of their arrival: some, like Mackay, would place it at the dawn of history (2600–2500 B.C.), while others follow H. Frankfort in thinking that it coincided with the beginning of Tell Obeid (4th millenium) as they are struck by the continuity of culture from the Obeid period until the predynastic age. However, a break was noticed by A. Parrot, J. Bottero and J. Jordan: the disappearance of painted pottery in lower Mesopotamia at the end of the Obeid period. The authors believe that this disappearance was due to the arrival of the Sumerians who, for a time, were unable to spread towards the north, as shown by the survival of painted pottery at Jemdet Nasr. In short, the problem has not yet been solved, nor has that of the Sumerians' place of origin. The oldest cultures of Hassuna (5th mill.), then those of Eridu in the south, and of Hassuna, Halaf and Samarra in the north (end of 5th and 4th millenium) show affinities with Iranian cultures, especially in their painted pottery. An Oriental origin would therefore not be out of the question, and this hypothesis is supported by other indications. Mythology, which might well have preserved the memory of ancient migrations, contains several references to the Orient: thus the goddesses of cereals, stock-breeding and weaving came down from the sacred mountains of the East for the greater benefit of Man. But even if we accept this theory of an Oriental origin unproved, we still do not know the starting point of the Sumerians. Philology has been unable to assign Sumerian to any specific group of languages, though one thing is certain: it belongs neither to a Semitic nor to an Indo-European family. An agglutinative language, it is formed mostly of monosyllabic words and has an unusual grammar that baffles the specialists; it has been compared with Chinese, though not conclusively, and with Zulu and Oceanian. But affinities are most likely to be found somewhere in ancient India, perhaps round the Indus valley or among the ancestors of the present Dravidians.

While archaeology has thus left unsolved these problems, which it has itself done much to raise, it has at least enabled us to formulate them, as H. Frankfort did in 1932. The increasing volume of archaeological discoveries has made it possible to assess and evaluate the data and to make better use of the whole of the evidence unearthed – pottery, tools, weapons, ornaments, and jewellery. Research has thus become both more limited and more extended: limited in the sense that the field of conjectures unsupported by material evidence is shrinking; and extended because the quantity of material is growing. Mistakes are still possible; thus when Baron Max von Oppenheim sought to date the bas-reliefs and sculptures of the Kaparra Palace (11th century B. C.) of Tell Halaf back to the 3rd millenium, he merely complicated an already difficult problem. But more or less reliable data are being obtained by the stratigraphic study of the various sites; this has made it possible to follow the progress of the Sumerians. Eridu, in view of its position on the Persian Gulf and of the privileged place it held in Sumerian mythology, would certainly have been the *point d'appui* of the invader, whether a whole people or – as seems more likely – relatively small groups of warriors. At the beginning they settled at Ur and Uruk and stayed there for a long time; once their domination had been consolidated, their civilizing influence – in the absence of an emigration proper – spread north by way of the rivers until it reached even Assyria.

A systematic examination of the area

The specific approach of 20th-century archaeology is well illustrated by the methodical and complete investigation of mounds: some have been abandoned only when it was realized that their exploration could be carried no further. This happened at Babylon where R. Koldewey spent eighteen consecutive years (1899–1917), day after day, clearing the buildings of the famous city, one after the other; this yielded relatively few items for museums but considerably increased our knowledge of architecture and town planning. Similar work was done on the ancient town of Susa – although this is outside the scope of this book – where the mound has been explored systematically by French teams since 1897. Sites investigated in the 19th century and subsequently abandoned have been reopened since improved techniques were bound to lead to fresh discoveries: at Dur-Sharrukin the Americans were able to establish an accurate plan, arrive at a better understanding of the town and bring to light some large sculptures; at Nineveh the British were able to determine the age of the site thanks to a dwelling of the third millenium and some painted potsherds.

Systematic research has also aimed at defining archaeologically the regions bordering on Mesopotamia proper, and work has been done in three main directions, north, east and west. In the east, a French team first investigated Elam whose territory, though near to it, must not be confused with that of Mesopotamia; despite continuous contacts – mostly military clashes – as is shown by the abundance of Mesopotamian documents found at Susa (such as the code of Hammurabi), and some trade relations, we are dealing with two completely distinct civilizations. In the valley of the Diyala, a tributary of the Tigris north-east of Baghdad, the sites of Tell Asmar, Khafaja, Tell Agrab and Ischeli have been studied; these were the main centres of the ancient kingdom of Eshnunna which had been searched for in vain in the 19th century. From 1930 on, the excavators of the Oriental Institute of Chicago, particulary H. Frankfort, S. Lloyd, P. Delougaz, Gordon Loud, and T. Jacobsen[10], were able to show that this rich and powerful kingdom of great antiquity, which was renowned even before the time of Sargon of Akkad and was the centre of an original art, was deservedly famous. Despite its somewhat remote position in relation to the great north-south axis, the valley of the Diyala cannot be considered apart from the development of Mesopotamia; but this is not the case with the regions situated in the north. The awareness that it was essential to an understanding of the complex interplay of influences, together with the proximity of Assyria, aroused the interest of scholars in this territory. Research work in the area has been slow and must still be considered unfinished, because of the numerous problems of chronological and ethnic demarcation at this meeting point between Asia Minor and the Mesopotamian world. Apart from the Assyrian sites of historic or protohistoric periods (Tepe Gawra, Tell Billa, Araptchiya), the first to attract attention were Tell Halaf (soundings 1899, excavations 1911–39, with interruptions, by the German archaeologist Max von Oppenheim) and Carlchemish, which has been excavated intermittently since 1876. Of the numerous mounds of the Khabur region, a crossroads between the south, Urartu and the Hittite country, and between the Mediterranean and Assyria, two were studied with especial care by the British excavator M. E. L. Mallowan: Chagar Bazar and Brak. Farther west, the excavations of Arslan-Tash (Hadatu) and Tell Ahmar (Til Barsib) by Thureau-Dangin, and Tell Atchana near the coast by Sir Leonard Woolley, enabled archaeologists to follow the east-west route which – in view of the great variety of influences – cannot yet be considered as completely explored. Finally, farther south, the middle course of the Euphrates yielded great discoveries: the exploration by mixed teams (American and French: Breasted, F. Cumont, M. Pullet, Clark Brown and M. du

Mesnil du Buisson) of Dura-Europos, a city of the Seleucid period and the first two centuries of the Christian era, provided a wonderful opportunity for the study of a synthesis of East and West. Then followed the systematic exploration – still in progress – of Tell Hariri (Mari), led since 1934 by A. Parrot, which completely revised our knowledge of the beginning of the 2nd millenium and added to our knowledge of the third millenium. Two features have distinguished the excavations of the last twenty years: the first, unfortunately, is the diminishing number of sites being explored. We can quickly summarize the main ones: besides the work done by A. Parrot, M.E.L. Mallowan and D. Oates, faithful to the traditional British interest in Assyria, have started to re-explore Balawat and Nimrud; the Germans, with H. Lenzen, are continuing the investigation of Warka and confirming the great importance of this Sumerian capital, and in 1955 Moortgat undertook the study of Fecherijeh; Nippur is being studied by American archaeologists led by Haines, while Braidwood is exploring the prehistoric sites (Jarmo, Muallafat, etc.)[11]. The second feature is the arrival of new countries in the field: the archaeologists of Syria and especially of Iraq are swelling the ranks of Orientalist scholars; excavations led by Naji Al Asil and Tacha Baqir have concentrated mainly on the sites of Aqarqug, Tell Harmal, Uqair and Hassuna; more recently, Hatra and the site of Bakr Awa (at present being excavated by Fuad Safar) have aroused the interest of the Iraqi authorities.

The place of Mesopotamia in the Oriental context

The excavations undertaken in the 20th century in the three great zones bordering on Mesopotamia have completely revised our views. They have sought to go beyond the traditional scope of research, and to determine the paths of influence and interaction between Iran, Caucasia, Anatolia, the Mediterranean countries and Mesopotamia. The Hurrians offer a good example of the complex difficulties met in the study and definition of a people. Having infiltrated into Upper Mesopotamia, doubtlessly in the second half of the third millenium, these newcomers, whose origin is uncertain, were definitely in evidence at the beginning of the second millenium, and by about 1500 B.C. formed the powerful State of Mitanni; its capital has not yet been found, but their domination has been proved archaeologically at Nuzi, Tell Brak, Alalakh, and their influence at Ugarit and at Mari. It is therefore necessary to define as accurately as possible what was their own contribution, what derived from an older Mesopotamian background and what they borrowed from neighbouring peoples. This cannot be established without much detailed and co-ordinated research work; nor is it unlikely that the problem will have to be reconsidered, in whole or in part, as a result of subsequent excavations.

Another striking example, which shows clearly how complex was the interplay of influences, is provided by the discovery of 10,000 Assyrian tablets dating from the beginning of the second millenium, in the midst of Hittite country at Kanesh (now Kultepe). These documents show the expansion of the Assyrians from the end of the third dynasty of Ur for more than two centuries, and how the rise of the first great Assyrian period which ended with Shamshi Adad I (1812–1780 B.C.) was due in part to extensive trading. They also illustrate the economic importance of the metal of Asia Minor during the Bronze Age and at the approach of the Iron Age. No doubt the raid of Sargon of Akkad (25th century B.C.) was prompted by the search for metal, and the building of a fortress at Tell Brak by Naram-Sin was undoubtedly due to the necessity to control the routes of access to metal, which had become indispensable for the maintenance of power.

In the field of Mesopotamia's external relations, the study of the ties uniting Mesopotamia and Iran during the protohistoric period is – as we have seen – far from complete. Despite their greater simplicity – which often is more apparent than real – the relations between Mesopotamia and Egypt have long been a subject of study. The points these two first great civilizations had in common – such as the similar geographical conditions in which they developed – were bound to interest an expert archaeologist like H. Frankfort. The use of similar decorative subjects in the first centuries (e.g., friezes of animals with inordinately elongated, interlacing necks) also suggests possible contacts. Diplomatic relations dating from historic times are mentioned in the chronicles and in the correspondence between Egyptian, Mitanian and Babylonian princes of the 14th century B.C., discovered at El Amarna in Egypt.

Finally, on the Mesopotamian sites themselves, 20th-century research has aimed at defining the extent of the influence exerted by the great cities. The ties linking the cities of the neo-Sumerian period, for instance, and their degree of dependency still remain to be elucidated. Why was Lagash, which had never been the seat of a dynasty, apparently more powerful than its neighbours under Gudea, or at least, why was it more brilliant than the others? Ur, for its part, claimed hegemony in Mesopotamia, and achieved it for a century: its influence spread as far as Persia, Elam, Armenia, Cappadocia and Syria.

Influence, however, can act two ways. That of Assyria radiated beyond Mesopotamia: its characteristics are reflected in the statuettes of men and animals in Urartu and in the jewellery of Sakiz, near Lake Urmia. But Assyria was also on the receiving end: this could not be better illustrated than by the collection of ivories found at Nimrud by M. E. L. Mallowan; some of these ornaments appear entirely Assyrian while others seem to continue the Anatolian, Syrian, Phoenician and even Egyptian traditions.

Problems of chronology

The complex play of influences has to be defined spatially. But 20th-century research has also aimed at defining its point in time. Recent discoveries have thrown doubt on the chronological conclusions reached in the 19th and at the beginning of the 20th century. First of all, the conquest of protohistory implied the establishment of a relative chronology by a comparative study of fourth- and third-millenium sites; as this developed in precision, the terminology of the different phases was modified and divergencies in the literature became apparent. In this field, the most noteworthy achievement of the last thirty years is the considerable shortening of the chronology of the historic period. As a result of excavations, particularly at Mari, an unexpected synchronism appeared between Hammurabi, King of Babylon, and King Shanshi Adad I of Assyria; this threw doubt on the dates customarily accepted for Hammurabi (2100–2000 B. C.). After a long study of the problem, it was found that the dates of the famous king of the first Babylonian dynasty had to be put forward by some three centuries, but no agreement was reached on a single set of dates. Three have been proposed. That suggested by Goetze, the long chronology, gives 1848–1806 for Hammurabi, but this is not generally followed. The second, or medium chronology, which seems to take into account the main data, has been suggested by S. Smith and

45

47

48

51

58 →

59

61

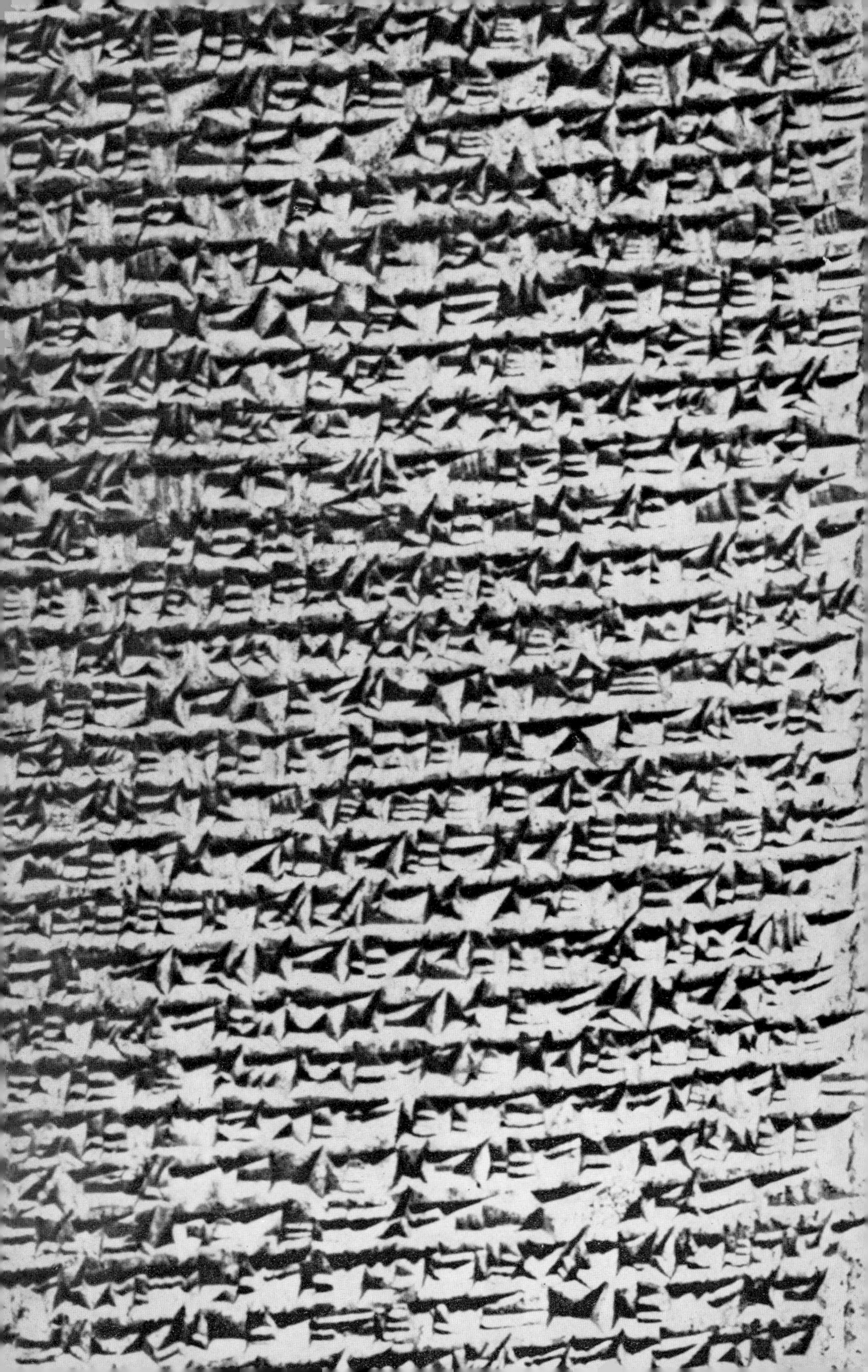

fixes Hammurabi's reign between 1792 and 1750; it is accepted by the French school, especially by A. Parrot, and by H. Frankfort and Sir Leonard Woolley. The last, or short chronology, suggested by W. F. Albright and accepted by some scholars, e.g., the German archaeologist H. Schmökel, assigns the years 1728–1686 to the Babylonian king. Thus we have a discrepancy of more than a century: some scholars take only the last two hypotheses into account and speak of a discrepancy of 60 years, which may still appear to be a great deal, but is not much when we consider the progress made since research was begun in this field. The period before this undecided date, from the beginning of the second millenium, can be considered accurate to within ten years in its relative, but not absolute, chronology. As we go back through the third millenium, the discrepancies attain a century or more; on the other hand, from the first Babylonian dynasty onwards, there is increasing accuracy, since we possess more and more documents which help chronological classification (lists of kings and eponyms of Assyria, Babylon and Elam, chronicles, inscriptions, etc). From the 16th century B.C. on, the absolute chronology is valid to within five years, and from the 10th there is no more chronological uncertainty. More detailed research has also been done into the transitional phases which had been neglected in favour of unified periods. These phases are extremely difficult to understand since they are marked by disturbances whose nature and influence are not completely known; attempts are being made, with the aid of archaeological and epigraphic evidence to dispel their obscurity. A recent study[12], based on the Mari tablets, has been made of the Amorite nomads who moved about the borders of the desert and formed part of that great Semite wave that overthrew the Mesopotamian world after the third dynasty of Ur, obtaining control of the great cities, both at Mari and Babylon. The world of a nomad people, which archaeology can never easily pin down because their traces are too ephemeral, has in this case been partially reconstituted; from the correspondence of the sovereigns of Mari we can get a better idea of the difficulties and dangers experienced by the urban communities.

The birth of a civilization

The direction taken by the investigations we have just briefly summarized is in the main historical and archaeological: it aims at giving a "profile" of each people and at discovering the military relations and economic ties between various regions. In addition, thanks to Sumer, Mesopotamia is an ideal place for studying the phenomenon of the birth of a civilization: "History begins at Sumer", wrote S. N. Kramer, the American Sumerologist. Moreover, while history begins at Sumer, Sumer also preceded history, i.e., the first written records; it thus poses the whole problem of the genesis of a civilization, of writing and of towns. One of the aims of archaeological research has therefore been to elucidate as clearly as possible the factors at the origin of the great discoveries of primitive man.

The new context in which this higher form of human life developed was the first feature to attract notice. After mastering the techniques of agriculture, man found metal, no doubt by chance. Moreover, during the Bronze Age civilization took a remarkable leap forward. Research has therefore been twofold. First, it has been devoted to the technical aspects: how did Man bridge the gulf between the discovery and utilization of metal, how did he learn to detect deposits and work them regularly, how did he learn to create the metal objects in more or less current use, going through the process of purifying ores and achieving an alloy? Where was metal discovered and in what regions was it first treated? How widely was it distributed? Other incidental questions arise; but we shall confine ourselves to saying that archaeologists, historians and technical experts are conducting intensive research to elucidate this essential stage in the development of a society[13] whose origins must, it seems, be looked for in Western Asia. A recent study[14] has shown the importance of metal-working in the first great Oriental civilization; without inventing it, the Sumerians indisputably achieved a level which had never previously been equalled, thanks in particular to the increasingly common use of metal tools. This led to a complete change in civilization, a transformation of economic and social structures, the growth of commercial relations, the birth of cities, the invention of writing, all linked in varying degrees to the major phenomenon of progress in metal-working, even though – and this is important – the Sumerians had to import metals since the alluvial soil of the valley of the two rivers obviously did not contain any ores.

The discovery of writing was fraught with as much consequence as the use of metal, and to it Sumer owed its supremacy in the East. Born of economic necessity, the invention of writing was undoubtedly due to an increase in agricultural production and the development of stock-farming within a social framework necessitating the presentation of accounts to owners living elsewhere. When production figures and the size of stocks could no longer be memorized, human ingenuity was challenged to find a substitute method; this was in the very distant past, in the middle of the Uruk period, i.e., a little before 3000 B.C. It is also possible that the growth of crafts and the new social structures that followed the appearance of metal may have led to this revolutionary discovery. Archaic tablets brought to light mainly at Kish, Jemdet Nasr and Shuruppak have enabled scholars of Sumerian to list the first signs of the script and their evolution; however, the conditions in which the first drawings evolved are not yet fully known and further discoveries are needed to establish them.

The third characteristic feature of Sumer was its organization into independent cities, more often than not jealous of one another, whose relations – still incompletely known – form the threads of history. Archaeological research aims at solving the fundamental problem of how and why the Neolithic village community with its pastoral and agricultural economy became a city with a complex economic structure. The town itself had a defensive appearance, thanks to its ramparts – there was no town without them – but this does not appear to be the decisive factor in its development. Some agree with Sir Leonard Woolley in thinking that it was due to improved organization of the land, which ensured crops by means of irrigation and thus an increase in wealth; cooperative work became necessary and the communal structures were enlarged until they attained urban stature. Others believe with A. Parrot that metallurgy was the main cause of the growth of cities, owing to a greater division of labour and a higher degree of specialization in the tasks required of each individual. This view, which appears closer to the truth, does not however completely exclude the first hypothesis.

Finally, the last and major aim of the 20th-century excavations has been the historians' legitimate desire to give everyone his due. Yet nothing could be more difficult in the Middle East; if we take an overall view of art alone, for instance, we are struck at first sight by the unity of the Mesopotamian world, even if slight differences from period to period do something to correct this summary impression. Differences may appear between one people and another: thus Assyrian art is more profane than that of Babylon or Sumer; but it is impossible, on this basis alone, to establish the mental, religious and artistic characteristics of all the peoples who lived in the country between the two rivers. Religion, which has always been the subject of careful study, does not enable us to distinguish between the Semitic contribution and Sumerian element. The date of the arrival of the Semites is no better known that that of the Sumerians; the pattern of an indigenous background submerged by a Sumerian wave that was halted by Sargon of Akkad (25th century B.C.), a sort of forerunner of the Semitic masses, is accepted only to simplify the problem. In reality, the Semites were settled in Mesopotamia before history recorded feats of their first great representative. They probably arrived at the same time as the Sumerians, or even before them, and from the fourth millenium until the Christian era other groups reinforced the first contingents; the Amorites (beginning of the second millenium), then the Aramaeans (end of the second millenium) came in relatively homogenous formations as is shown by archaeological and epigraphic discoveries. In fact, there was a slow and more or less continous infiltration of nomads from the Arabic peninsula. Other peoples, such as the Gutis, the Kassites and even the Hurrians, left their mountains to settle in the country of the two rivers. The fusion of all these peoples gave birth to the Sumero-Assyro-Babylonian civilization, a synthesis of various tendencies in which it is difficult to distinguish the part played by each one; nevertheless, persevering study[15] has cleared up a number of points.

There are still a number of problems whose solution is not yet in sight and of working hypotheses that have not yet been verified; some of them have been raised by archaeology, and archaeology alone can solve them; others will require the joint work of all the historical disciplines. Even if one day we approach a solution, archaeological research will not be ended: the tens of thousands of tablets waiting in museums to be read and translated will raise new questions to which excavations may find the answer. The pre-Sargon palace found at Mari during the 1964 expedition and now being cleared, the large number of mounds in Mesopotamia that have not yet been sounded – these give us hope that certain notable towns (e.g. Akkad) that have so far remained hidden from the excavator may yet be found.

The specialist in Mesopotamian archaeology may still look forward to great discoveries.

METHODS OF MESOPOTAMIAN ARCHAEOLOGY

IV

In Mesopotamia, as elsewhere, archaeology did not develop in a day. Slowly, site by site, through contact with allied sciences, such as prehistory and geology, that were also trying to read the message of the buried past, the rules that govern it took shape during the 19th and 20th centuries.

Changes in excavation techniques

The travellers who collected objects from the surfaces of mounds were certainly not archaeologists, and we even hesitate to give that title to the first excavators whose aim – and this was the characteristic feature of the earliest phase – was primarily to find and bring back to Europe art objects and tablets; but can we blame them for their lack of "archaeological conscience"? They were, for the most part, subsidised by English or French museums, whose only concern was to add to their collections. They had clear orders: to bring back objects. Besides, the science of archaeology had not yet developed sufficiently to teach them that the soil could yield infinitely more than a series of art objects to enrich the showcases of museums. Although no tested method was known, some archaeologists nevertheless excavated less badly than others. The worst of all was H. Rassam, an Oriental Christian, who literally pillaged mounds on behalf of Britain, with no concern whatever for methodical research; for many years he tore through the country, systematically rifling as many sites as possible. Admittedly, he reaped a splendid harvest–but at what cost. It is impossible to tell with any degree of accuracy where any of the objects came from or the context in which they were found; sites were completely ravaged, buildings overthrown. His procedure was simple: to make straight for the object by digging a hole. Compared with this disastrous method, that of archaeologists like Botta, who dug tunnels, seems to have been almost perfect. With few exceptions, such as V. Place who took advantage of the presence of an architect to obtain accurate surveys of the excavated buildings, most excavators searched simply for objects.

At the end of the 19th century, methods began to be more systematic, and it became clear that excavation demanded strict rules. The tunnelling procedure had already been abandoned by Sarzec, who lined up his workers and made them take soundings yard by yard. While this method is open to critism, it did at least enable him to gain an overall idea of the site. Misconceptions had to be dispelled before any appreciable progress could be made; sites in the Sumer country which appeared to have been occupied for particularly long periods were tackled against the advice of the Assyriologist Hilprecht, precht, who considered that a long succession of dwellings in one place would necessarily wipe out ancient traces of settlement. Meanwhile, the first stratigraphic studies were made on high-lying sites; this great step was first taken by the German archaeologist Koldewey at Surghul in 1887. Along the whole length of the site he laid out a trench thirty feet wide at the top. The different levels could thus be seen; he could not yet draw all the possible conclusions from them, but the principle had been established andapplied and it led to the use of more exact methods even though the procedure was later an considerably modified. A trained architect, Koldewey also made his mark on Mesopotamian archaeology by a systematic clearing of horizontal levels at Babylon so that he could obtain an overall view of the site and study its broad outlines. In the course of his various excavations he perfected his methods, and it may be said that in the first quarter of this century the methods available to archaeologists in the Middle East were capable of yielding fruitful results. However, the wealth of evidence that could be obtained from stratigraphic exploration was not fully recognized, and it was a long time before some of the excavators of the old school really applied this new method, though it is certain that protohistoric sites could never have yielded so much information without it. Fortunately, Koldewey had pupils such as Andrae, the excavator of Assur, who perfected his methods and applied a new precision to Oriental archaeology.

The preparatory phase

The laymen tends to think of archaeology as a vast undertaking aimed at unearthing vestiges of the past, and is interested only in the actual excavations; in fact, preparatory research is now considered essential to the success of the operation. Research alone, with the aid of all available sources of information, can determine and delimit the future working site. Until this century, excavations were most frequently begun by chance – as at Tello and originally at Mari – as a result of an archaeologist's individual flair, or following the appearance of some especially interesting items – generally tablets found in clandestine excavations – on the antique market. Then excavations were begun – if the site could be found – for fear that its essential features might disappear under the pickaxes of vandals or be pillaged and lost for ever. Sometimes, too, a site whose name seemed to be derived from that of an ancient town attracted attention, as was the case with Nineveh and Babylon. We must admit that for a century fortune seems to have smiled on archaeologists since some first-class sites were discovered by chance; in any case, no other means were available at that time – there are so many mounds in the Orient, after over six millenia of human occupation, that a systematic excavation of every one of them is as impossible today as it was in the past. Although over the last hundred and fifty years an increasing number of exploratory expeditions have made rapid soundings or prospected the surface, there are still innumerable mounds of which we know nothing at all.

Until quite recently, the only way to study the archaeological value of a region was to go there; it was necessary to be able to "see with one's own eyes". While this is still essential, aerial photography can now, in the preparatory phase, enable the archaeologist to limit the field of enquiry and to direct the research work more accurately. This technique, which is now in common use in Europe, has not been exploited fully in Mesopotamia; yet aerial reconnaissance made at certain times and in certain conditions of humidity would greatly facilitate the drawing up of an archaeological map for the whole of the Middle East. In Iraq, this is now being done and, the ancient network of canals is also being studied by the same method. The techniques of scientific prospecting (measuring resistibility, magnetic methods, etc.) do not seem to have much future on the Mesopotamian type of soil, for the architectural remains – which are the most important for this type of investigation – by their very nature are merged with the soil.

After defining the object of the investigation very precisely, archaeologists must use all available information on the region so that nothing is left to chance. It was thus that Sir Leonard Woolley came to choose the mound of Atchana as the site of his excavation. The choice of this mound, situated among at least two hundred similar ones in the plain of Amq which is crossed by the Orontes, was the outcome of a carefully thought-out plan to bring to light a site that would, through the cross-section of material remains, yield information in chronological sequence on the economic and cultural relations between

Mesopotamia and the Mediterranean. It was in order to specify level I of Tell Hassuna and to study the phase of domestication of plants (barley, wild corn) and of animals (pigs, cows, horses) that Braidwood and his team of botanists and zoologists – after a fruitless attempt at Matarra – chose the site of Jarmo, which had already been prospected by S. Lloyd and Fuad Safar in 1945. These are excellent examples of methodical research carried out on the basis of perfectly defined working hypotheses.

It is not surprising that these prospecting methods are not yet universally used in their entirety: there still are, and always will be, chance discoveries, just as there are mounds demanding systematic exploration. Moreover, the main outlines of the archaeological past had at first to be found by "chance" in order that an archaeological technique could subsequently be founded on a scientific basis; after all, every science has had to go through an empirical phase.

Conditions of excavation peculiar to Mesopotamia

The second phase of archaeological exploration in Mesopotamia is not the same as in western countries; first of all, the more extreme climate may naturally play a part in the choice of the site, and always determines the time of year chosen for an expedition. Admittedly, the whole of Mesopotamia is not like Sumer where heat, hot sand-carrying winds,[16] drought or flood combine to make work particularly difficult; but while conditions in the upper and middle part of the country are less severe, they never really allow perfect freedom of movement. The soil, too, has influenced the work of the archaeologist. Formed by the progressive silting-up of a large gulf with alluvial deposits from two great rivers that finally converged, the clayey soil of Mesopotamia is of inexhaustible wealth both for agriculture – as the first human groups in the Neolithic age fully realized – once it is irrigated, and for the manufacture of everyday objects, once it is fashioned, moulded and fired so as to be solid enough to withstand long use.

With very few exceptions, clay was the basic material of all Mesopotamian buildings. Mostly it was used practically unchanged: either as it was, or with an addition of chopped straw to give it better cohesion, it was formed into mud bricks that were dried in the sun. Fired bricks were used only in special cases, e.g., for paving or – more often – as a

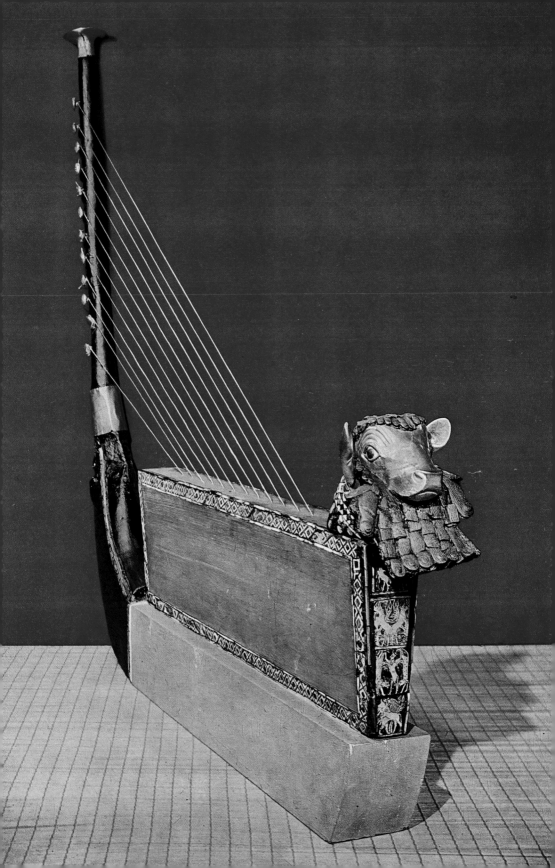

64, 65

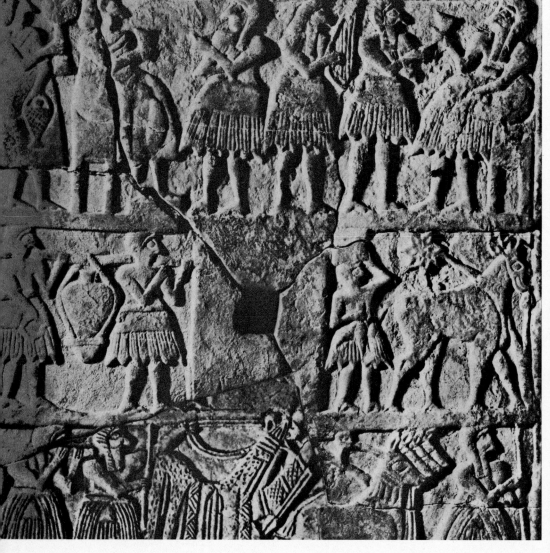

75

77, 78 →

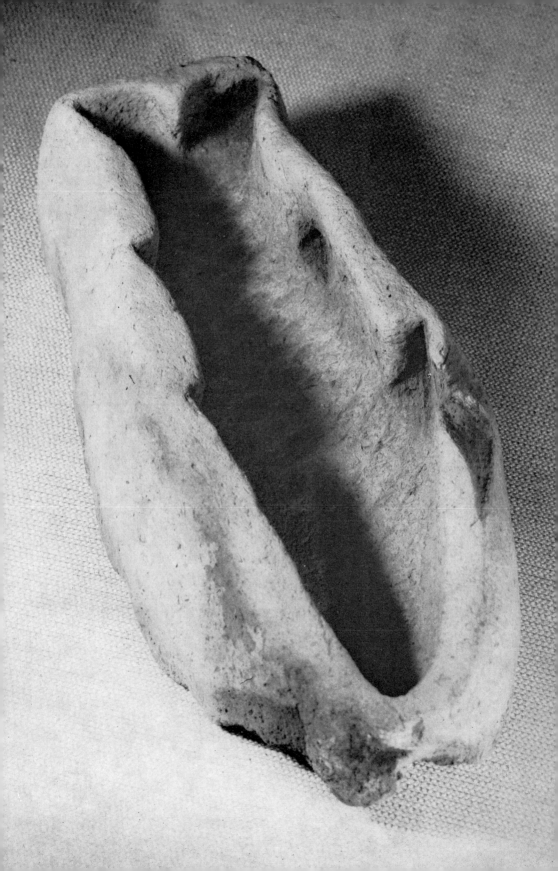

facing on large buildings to give them greater solidity; this form of facing was used more frequently in the late period and was responsible for the partial preservation to this day of the gate of Ishtar at Babylon where it was covered with a layer of enamel and used as much as an architectural decoration as to protect the walls. It was rarely manufactured because of the scarcity of fuel in the region; this is a pity, for Mesopotamia could have had an even greater wealth of imposing buildings than Egypt and Greece.

The usual building material was thus fragile and ephemeral; a mud-brick building lasted as long as its protective covering, and then only if the foundation of its walls was not being sapped by rain water. A slight crack in the terraced roof would lead to the disintegration of the wall which would return to its original state, i.e., mud. An ordinary building would last a dozen years, sometimes less. Only special buildings receiving regular care and maintenance, such as temples or palaces, could hope for a longer life span, and even so, an amazing number of temples had to be completely rebuilt: eighteen successive states of rebuilding, without counting partial restoration, were found in one temple at Eridu. As the result of general use or wilful destruction (e.g., fire which might be accidental but more often followed military conquest, demolition to make way for a better building) a building would deteriorate and the foundations of the walls became buried under the collapsed upper parts; where erosion did not remove it, the soil from disintegrated bricks protected the foundations. In rebuilding, the surface was simply smoothed over; in fact, it would have been too much work to clear the rubble, and the resulting slight elevation had the advantage of insulating the building from the underlying water layer which was still very close. Once the surface was levelled, new foundations were dug which did not always go down to the level of the previous foundations when there was a thick layer of rubble. In other cases, where a new plan was adopted, this sometimes cut across the old foundations; but when the plan was unchanged, the walls were simply used again. In short, where the foundation works were not too deep, the earlier soil became, as it were, fossilized; there are cases, however, in which terracing works undertaken since ancient times have removed the first layers and the archaeologist finds to his disappointment that he cannot study the evolution of the building. However, it is generally possible to follow the successive stages. Each layer – which must not be confused with an age or a period – can be classified if several soils are found. Moreover, thanks to the remains – however scanty – they contain, the successive layers of soil yield a great deal of information on the evolution of an environment and the conditions peculiar to the period. Archaeological excavation, used with subtlety, can obtain extremely accurate information and reconstruct the glories and vicissitudes of a building, a a town, and even a whole region.

After centuries and millenia, the accumulated evidence of man's activities can attain impressive dimensions – up to 70 feet and occasionally, as at Tell Brak, to more than 140 feet. Admittedly, the height has little bearing on the interest of a site, especially now that the fundamental data on the history of the Middle East have been obtained; an imposing mound may add very little to our knowledge; conversely, an apparently insignificant site may prove of paramount importance. If the excavators Mackay and Langdon had looked only for height, the site of Jemdet Nasr, whose 12 feet seemed very small compared to the 56 feet at Kish, would never have attracted their notice.

Whatever the height of the mound, the principle that remains true for all human settlements is that the vestiges of life and industry pile up and are buried with the passing of the centuries; the height increases from generation to generation until the day when the site is abandoned and natural erosion takes over. The mound confronting the excavator faithfully reflects the chronological order of events from top to bottom. This principle, demonstrated by geology and prehistory, does not apply only to the Orient, but there it finds striking confirmation because of the nature of the material. It is at the basis of stratigraphic excavation, making it possible to understand the whole evolution of a site and, by comparison with other mounds in the area, to discover the human changes in a region.

In Mesopotamia this method has as many difficulties as advantages, owing to the nature of the terrain. Research is easy in one way, because it is possible to penetrate, level by level, down to virgin soil, without any danger of being stopped by monumental works of art in stone or any other material that might withstand the inclemency of the weather once brought to light. But this apparent ease is a snare: no other sites are more difficult to excavate than those in the Middle East where the presence of a wall is not shown by piled-up stones but simply by a very slight difference in colouring which can be discerned only after long practice. It is particularly difficult to recognize a wall from a crumbled fragment, and even more when it has reverted to clay and mud. It is therefore hardly surprising that the first Mesopotamian excavators had such difficulty in distinguishing architectural features that, before daring to speak of a wall, they waited in the hope of finding a row of stone bas-reliefs, and that it took a long apprenticeship before the soils and walls could be distinguished from heaps of earth.

The final difficulty occurs when the mound stands above a water layer or when – as in the Sumer country – the plain turns into a marsh at high water; in that case, the lower archaeological layers are often on a level with the infiltrating water and the work cannot be continued. There is no question of distinguishing levels in what has become a veritable quagmire and all that can be hoped is to save remains without being able to determine their origin with any accuracy or to place them chronologically. Despite the difficulties peculiar to Mesopotamian archaeology and the different methods employed (e.g., horizontal trenching, stratigraphic boring), it must be stressed that certain definite conclusions have been reached. In more than a century of excavations the number and value of these conclusions have fundamentally modified the whole archaeological approach: on the one hand, the object no longer forms the ultimate goal of research, on the other, the archaeologist in the field is able to use all kinds of data which previously seemed without interest. In 1849 Layard abandoned the site of Tepe Gawra because he had found nothing but potsherds there; it was the very presence of these potsherds that induced Speiser to choose the site in 1927. This clearly illustrates how methods have developed.

A special feature: the presence of texts

One of the features that differentiates Mesopotamia considerably from the other archaeological regions is that excavation there, more easily than elsewhere, may reveal to us the way the ancient peoples thought and acted, thanks to the existence of texts. The first of these texts – and perhaps the greatest – was the Old Testament whose importance in handing down the memory of the Ninevite and Babylonian Empires was discussed above. But to be on reliable ground, Orientalism had to detach itself from the

Bible and not to let itself become enslaved by it, however valuable a source it might be. Fossey's warning at the begining of the century shows that this was not always easy,[17] and the public often took an interest in Oriental archaeology only in so far as it confirmed the Scriptures. However, thanks to the thousands of tablets found, interest in the Orient grew considerably, and the disciplines of archaeology and epigraphy could develop at an equal pace. On many sites the presence of an epigraphist was considered essential in order to obtain a first reading of the inscriptions which might guide the immediate research; and while the written documents could be of help to the archaeologist on the spot, they were of even greater use when their subsequent translation and study could clarify the general direction research should take. Thus, from the time of the first teams, Orientalists such as R. Dussaud, E. Dhorme, R. Labat, G. Dossin, J. Nougayrol, N. S. Kramer, A. Falkenstein and W. von Sonden, have continually furnished archaeologists with new data for their research. Some, like G. Contenau, have even combined or are combining the two activities. However, the texts do not reveal the whole truth about the ancient world, any more than does archaeology alone; the two disciplines complement one another and form part of the historical method. Even if one appears only to confirm the other, they constitute two very different approaches to the past. Archaeology alone cannot enable us to understand the thought of the ancient world, but it supplies an image of the tangible, concrete, material features of a civilization, and shows man's means and possibilities in controlling his environment. It is the sole source for the protohistoric periods and as such irreplaceable; but it is also essential in the study of the historic periods – if only by discovering the texts.

Archaeology: a sum total of disciplines

Archaeology, therefore, does not aim solely at unearthing evidence – important though this may be; it tries, above all, to recapture the way peoples lived. To this end, the archaeologist must be able to distinguish, understand and explain all the facets of the life of a lost society. He needs a great variety of knowledge: archaeological knowledge and general culture cannot be separated when it comes to associating apparently independent facts, and such associations are often the source of new hypotheses and fruitful research.

The Mesopotamian archaeologist must know his Bible, and – without necessarily becoming a philologist – must have some idea of the philology of Semitic and Sumerian languages. While he needs a solid grounding in the various auxiliary disciplines, he does not have to replace the experts. A rudimentary knowledge of physical, economic and human geography is required to understand the natural environment and its exigencies, the possibilities of changes in a region and their effect on the human environment, such as the decrease that has almost certainly occurred in the rainfall of the Middle East in the course of four millenia. At any stage of the research work, during the excavations as well as afterwards, these allied sciences come into play; they enable the archaeologist to cope with any problems and to be at all times fully in charge of the process of discovery.

To an experienced scholar the discovery of a simple cylinder on a site can convey a wealth of information. Its style, its decorative motifs, its state of decay, the manner of the intaglio, etc., will help him to date the item, and this may subsequently enable him to assign a chronological classification to the layer where the object was found. But the cylinder is much more than a simple means of dating: it is evidence of the art of a period and, above all, a memento of the life of a man, of a type of human relations and of a special conception of property. All this can be gleaned from a small roll of carved stone! In the same way, the archaeologist must have a knowledge of pottery, which enables him to approach a civilization at a more humble level. In most cases, pottery objects are found only in the form of abundant debris, testifying to local production. Where they achieve the level of an article for export and have intrinsic qualities of finish and beauty, they become a prime factor in the study of the relations between human groups. The common utensils in Mesopotamia, where there was never any lack of clay, were not objects of this kind; they were made by craftsmen rather than artists and are interesting mainly for their technique, though occasionally they delight us with evidence of a certain artistic feeling, even if this was inhibited by the religious or social concepts of the time. Pottery is not only a means of understanding the technique and the art of a given period, but an essential – perhaps the best – means of dating, since the development of a certain type of vase, shape or ornament can be followed with great accuracy. In short, the distribution of different types of pottery and decorative motifs is extremely helpful in the study of a given human group, and especially valuable in the absence of texts covering the archaic periods.

Topography, metal-working techniques, sculpture, architecture, painting and anthropology: knowledge in all these fields is constantly being called to the aid of Mesopotamian archaeology. It is also necessary to know how to protect items that do not easily withstand being taken out of the earth and are in a particularly critical state at the time of their discovery. Plastering and paraffining processes are frequently used, as for example in collecting and transporting the lions of the temple of Dagan at Mari, and in recovering the forms of the harps at Ur (the wood had disappeared, but not the decoration encrusted in it). The removal of paint is another particularly delicate operation for which a specialist has to be called in, as at Dura-Europos and at Mari. Numerous finds have to undergo further treatment on their arrival at the museum to ensure their perfect preservation.

This is usually the moment when the archaeologist may have recourse to laboratories and experts to clarify certain points; human bones are often handed on to anthropologists who can identify ethnic characteristics. It is also possible – although this process is not much used – to study the thermo-residual magnetization of fired clay by intensifying such studies it becomes possible to obtain chronological data. Carbon 14 or radioactive carbon which is contained in all living matter also makes it possible to date with some accuracy, especially for the ancient periods: thanks to the carbon 14 method the age of the Jarmo site has been lowered from 6000 to 4857, with a margin of error (plus 320 years) which is insignificant in this case but might invalidate the method for more recent periods.

Once the excavation is finished the archaeologist must publish his findings without delay, whatever their apparent importance, so that all can benefit from them. Such accounts must be as accurate, detailed and as complete as possible, for it is the archaeologist's aim to supply the materials of history. More often the archaeologist himself turns historian; basing himself on all the mementos of the past, he publishes monographs, studies of details and then syntheses which add to our total knowledge of a region or a period. Thus, it took years to establish an exact Mesopotamian chronology in relation to Hammurabi – and, as we have seen, the results are not yet final – with the aid of texts, lists of kings, correspondence between sovereigns of different regions (Babylonia, the kingdom of Mari and Eshnunna), astronomical research (some texts referred to observations of the planet Venus) and agreements and disagreements in the ceramic series of Hammurabi, of his neighbours and of his successors (Kassites). An investigation of this scope, which combines astronomical data with the evaluation of written documents and pottery, can be contrasted with the more purely archaeological study of Mesopotamian protohistory. On the basis of the first architectural remains, tools, weapons and pottery, by studying similarities and dissimilarities, by establishing sequences capable of revealing breaks or continuity, and by constant reference to stratigraphic data, it has been possible to achieve a partial resurrection of two millenia of human life, although the task is not yet complete. Thanks to the progress made, Mesopotamian chronology has been used as a standard reference for Mediterranean countries.

Some people have been surprised – even shocked – at the scientific character archaeology has assumed in this century and have accused it of losing sight of its main objective: the rediscovery of man as he was at a certain phase in his evolution — as if a report on an excavation or a study of pottery or bronze-working ceased to be within the scope of archaeology as soon as other technical, scientific or mathematical skills were called to its aid. But such reproaches are pointless. In the first stage of this "discovery of buried worlds" a silhouette of ancient man appeared, but the outlines remained ill-defined, the face blurred, the limbs unclear, as in the first rough outline by a sculptor. Now the second phase is beginning, a more difficult, slower, more complex process during which the image is being defined more clearly: only rigorously scientific methods can, stroke by stroke, make the face of ancient man emerge from the twilight of the ages.

Divine or royal couple. Provincial art of Upper Khabur, Tell Halaf. Beginning of the 1st millennium. Basalt.
Height: 31 inches. Width: 35 inches. Aleppo Museum.

THE SETTING OF LIFE

The great achievement of more than a century of archaeology on Mesopotamian soil is to have uncovered a civilization that was able to settle, develop and renew itself for more than four millenia. At the moment of the first stroke of the pickaxe on an Oriental mound no one dreamed of the incomparable intellectual and artistic wealth that would be revealed. Not only a people, but a whole complex world was resurrected, for despite an apparent uniformity, there was no real unity: each wave of invasion, from prehistory to the Medes and Persians, made its own contribution. But it would be a hazardous undertaking to attempt in a few pages to evaluate each of these contributions; some of the greatest scholars, after devoting a lifetime to this study, still hesitate to make any definite pronouncement. But if there was no real unity, there was nevertheless a synthesis of different contributions in thought and religion. In this, as in other matters, Mesopotamia has been a veritable melting-pot, and notwithstanding the originality of the Sumerians and the Akkadians, the numerous points of resemblance between the peoples who inhabited the region are more striking than the divergencies.

Mesopotamian archaeology, however, suffers from an incurable disadvantage: it cannot point to majestic buildings resplendent in the sun, it has no Parthenon, no Hadrian's Villa, no temple of Abu-Simbel, no island of Philae. The most perishable material was used, and any archaeological ensemble brought to light is doomed to certain destruction. When a layman has the good fortune to be able to visit a building on a site just after it has been cleared, he is disappointed by the clay walls; the size cannot always make up for the lack of brilliance once the façades have lost their whitewash. Babylon, a city whose renown has spanned millenia, is again reverting to dust after the Koldewey expedition tried to reconstruct it faithfully; only the gate of Ishtar has been able to withstand the ravages of the weather, thanks to its covering of enamelled bricks.[18] One of the best preserved buildings, the palace of Mari, has deteriorated considerably over some twenty-five years: the unearthed walls are again crumbling and forming fresh mounds which the weather is levelling. There are thus few, if any, buildings that recall the past[19]; there are some small fragments in the shelter of museums, the material made public by excavators and some attempts at reconstruction without which – despite every effort of the imagination – the work of archaeologists would remain a dead letter to most.

As he delves into the life of past civilizations, the archaeologist uncovers both the common-place and the unexpected: how can we fail to be moved on seeing the paw-prints of a dog that ran by chance across drying bricks, or the fingerprints so often made on fired bricks to increase the cohesion of the mortar. Our imagination takes wing when, as at Mari, we find, in a courtyard close to the entrance gate of the palace, the markings of a game whose rules we cannot know but which occupied the off-duty hours of the guards; in the same palace there is still charcoal in the kitchen furnaces which were extinguished on the day of massacre when all life left the palace for ever. Sometimes the excavator stumbles upon mementos of events that were splendid, moving and horrible in their cruelty: we can imagine Sir Leonard Woolley's feelings when he brought to light the famous royal tombs of Ur, sixteen altogether, which illustrated the practice of collective sacrifices, whether voluntary or not, when a person of royal blood died. Among them was the tomb of Queen Shub-ad who lay, with her ornaments and jewels, in the midst of her fur-nishings of precious metal. In front of the vault in which she lay alone was an ante-chamber containing the skeletons of soldiers, ladies-in-waiting, grooms and two donkeys attached to her chariot: the whole suite that accompanied the dead queen on her last great journey. In another tomb, called "the great well of death", the vault containing the royal body has not been found, but seventy-four people were there to accompany it, mostly women, whose bodies were laid out in rows, the legs slightly bent, and dressed in their most beautiful finery (red coats). Twenty-eight of them were wearing golden bands round their heads, and careful clearance work showed that the others had worn silver ones which had not withstood corrosion; the carts, oxen, lyres, and weapons were found in such order that we may suppose that this suite sacrificed itself voluntarily to follow its master. We can also deduce that they did not die a brutal death; it was probably caused by a poison which was taken in the vault itself and took effect after each had taken her place with her musical instruments, weapons and jewels; at least, there is no trace of resistance. We must assume that, after death had completed its work, someone went down to the tomb to check the positions of the bodies, for everything was in perfect order. However, a detail observed by the perceptive excavator adds a note of the unexpected: one of the women did not have her silver band on her head, and it was found under her body, at the level of her hand, flattened and out of shape. The excavator deduced that she arrived late for the ceremony with no time to put her band on her head and that she just had time to slip into her place before the fatal moment. Whether this was so or not, small facts of this kind introduce a human element into the most tragic scenes. There are many more examples, but none more moving perhaps than this – admittedly exceptional – insight into a very distant past. These tombs have also yielded mementos of an art that had achieved outstanding delicacy and truth, such as the helmet of Meskalamdug, jewels, rams mounted on bushes, and decorated lyres. As well as making such exceptional and fascinating discoveries, the archaeologist has laboured patiently to reconstitute the everyday environment of a Sumerian living in the town of Ur in the third millenium, of an Akkadian of the time of Zimri-lim, King of Mari, or of Hammurabi of Babylon in the second millenium, and of an Assyrian warrior of Assurbanipal in the 7th century.

The normal setting of life in Mesopotamia was the city; not that the whole of the sedentary population lived there, but the city with its religious and civic buildings and its administrative function formed the vital centre for each region, round which all its activities revolved. This was primarily because the town was constantly gaining in height by being rebuilt on its rubble, and with its imposing buildings it dominated the surrounding countryside. But the city could not live by itself: the entire neighbourhood was utilized to supply its food and basic needs. The soil had to be irrigated to counteract the long dry season; this irrigation system, which was started in the most distant past, transformed the country of the two rivers into the Eden which the nomadic Semites and the mountain people of the Zagros coveted. An increasingly complex and skilful network of canals fed by the rivers brought water, the essential source of life, to the remotest field; through strict control all parts of the land were regularly supplied. The need for water sometimes led to extensive public works: in the 8th century, Sennacherib impounded a source more than 30 miles from Nineveh and brought the water by pipes, a tunnel and an aqueduct (Jerwan, five stone arches over a length of 300 yards and a width of 22 yards) to the capital.

But the Mesopotamian soil had not been transformed entirely into fields; the marshes, especially in lower Mesopotamia, occupied vast spaces that were used for hunting and fishing. An Assyrian bas-relief from Nineveh, which depicts a battle in the marshes, shows fish and crabs in the water and a wild sow hiding in the rushes with her young. In the

Sumer period, a part of the population, though free, was obliged to supply the temple with a certain quantity of fish caught in the marshes or canals. There were many fishermen and others living outside the city in reed or palm huts – for the palm was the only tree that grew freely in the country – or in small puddled-clay houses. Such dwellings have been found either near fields or near reserves, pasture-lands, fenced-in paddocks and cattle-sheds, such as are shown on the cylinders; these protected the cattle, not from the weather but from the many wild beasts that roamed the country (wild bulls, jackals, hyenas, wild boars and lions[20]). This whole countryside was bustling with activity, for it was hard work to grow barley, raise cattle and draw milk, as can be seen from the bas-relief of the "dairy" from the temple of Tell Obeid. The produce had then to be loaded and taken by the canals to the town, or packed on to asses and carts. The trip was made preferably in groups, and on the way the country people would stare at the caravans of merchants who had often come a long distance to bring the precious and exotic goods for which civilization had created a need; like the peasants, these merchants worked only for this civilization to which, infact, they owed their existence.

The city evolved in the course of Mesopotamian history: it started off without a plan and at first grew empirically as the need arose. In the Assyrian period (end of the 8th century), Sargon wanted to change his capital and build one at Dur-Sharrukin with some attempt at town planning; while the plan was not as regular as those of the Hellenistic cities at a later date, there was a clear overall layout.

In the early days of the Sumerian period the city was organized round a central core, the temple. In the period of Mesilim of Kish (c. 2600 B.C.) a second core was formed by the palace which subsequently eclipsed the temple in importance; from that time till the end of Mesopotamian history, the palace and the temple were the two poles round which was organized the life of the city and soon of the empire itself. The data obtained from the soil have made up for the sparseness of texts for some periods and for their absence for others, since the remains of buildings brought to light can sometimes instruct us on the social organization and even on the nature of the government.

In this respect, the clearing of the temple of Khafaja has been particularly valuable since its plan clearly reveals its dual function: it was first of all a place of worship, and the central position of the *cella* which is on a raised terrace, at least 20 feet high, and separate from all the other structures, demonstrates the importance of its role in this respect; but it was also the economic centre of the city, since shops and workshops were found there. Through religion and trade, the temple thus provided a link between the people of the community; at its head, a priest-king (called *ensi* or *patesi* in Sumerian) was the representative, the vicar of the god in the city and its territory; he was helped in the administration of his domain by scribes who kept strict daily accounts of all the dues the people owed the temple, and who compiled the archives.

But towards the 25th century B.C. a basic change occurred in the structure of the State: side by side with the temple, which was no longer the sole centre, appeared the palace – this first occurred, it seems, at Kish in the time of Mesilim, i.e., at the very moment when the first written documents mark the beginning of history. It is difficult to determine what circumstances led to the secularization of power; but this evolution continued, and by the beginning of the second millenium the sovereigns' palace had become the real centre of the city. Brutally destroyed at the height of its prosperity by Hammurabi, the palace of Mari is a good example of the function of these royal buildings and the role they assumed. Of this monumental complex, A. Parrot brought to light 260 rooms and corridors out of the 300 it must have contained (the south-east corner has completely disappeared). It occupied an area of more than six acres in the very heart of the city and was not only a royal residence but the veritable nerve centre of the town and the kingdom; in it, administration, economy and religion all occupied an important place. Besides the royal apartments, the reception halls and courtyards and the apartments of high officials, whole sections were occupied by an army of officials, by the economic and diplomatic archives, the guardrooms, the schools of scribes, kitchens, workshops and shops. The sovereign could rule the whole kingdom from his apartment through his agents. Like the temple of the Sumerian period, the palace was partly bound up with the economy, and its workshops supplied more than just its own maintenance. Despite the secularization of the government, which was real but never total, the sovereign did not forget his sacerdotal functions; the palace contained chapels which in Assyria – for instance, in the palace of Sargon at Dur-Sharrukin – formed a whole section. The people always saw a connexion between the prosperity of the kingdom and the fulfilment of certain religious rites by the king.

The temples were often situated in the vicinity of the palace and formed veritable cultural zones round the ziggurat: the storeyed towers, so typical of the ancient East, did not yet exist in or near the city in early Sumerian times, but there were temples that stood on high terraces. The traditional building progressively diminished in size, and its place was taken by the ziggurat, generally consisting of a series of terraces which grew successively smaller; a small shrine stood at the top. Every sizeable urban centre had its own tower; in that country of wide horizons, where objects stand out clearly against the sky in certain lights, it gave each city its individual outline. The massive, imposing and solemn ziggurats, whose height sometimes exceeded 160 feet (300 feet at Babylon), shone dazzlingly in the eastern sun. Their vivid colours were arranged from the base upward, in the order of white, black, red, purple, and blue; sometimes other shades, like yellow or grey, were included, and there is no doubt that the colours had a religious significance. Shrines were sometimes set up in other parts of the town, but the ziggurat and the main temples comprised a veritable sacred zone and sometimes, as at Ur, a holy city. On feast days this religious centre, which was inhabited by the priests and the servants of the deities, was thronged with the faithful; on ordinary days there was no crowd, but sacrifices were performed at the request of individuals and libations offered as a ritual routine, so that it always was a busy part of the town.

Besides the temples and palaces, the city contained houses which were usually rather small except when they were residences of the rich and powerful. The rooms were laid out, according to the plan customary at the time, round a courtyard which gave them light; an inner or outer staircase led to the first-floor rooms or to the terraced roof where it was pleasantly cool in the evening after the overwhelming heat of the day. Some houses – although this was rare in the city – were only huts of reeds hidden under a layer of mud. The streets were bordered by blind, whitewashed walls and were usually not very wide: an ox-drawn cart could go through them easily, but could not always pass another; They were sometimes paved irregularly, especially when they led to a sanctuary; but when they were not and did not even have a simple layer of gravel, they became quagmires during the rains. They were busy streets, bustling with peasants who had come to sell their corn or cattle and merchants crying their wares; weavers, cutters, tanners, sculptors, engravers of cylinders and precious stones, potters, metal-workers were all to be found there in their stalls, their shops or under their awnings, calling to passing customers, idlers, servants or slaves. Life was busiest round the waterways where goods were being loaded, unloaded or stored in sheds. Farther from the town centre the houses were spaced out and surrounded by gardens. Then came the mighty town walls, reinforced by towers, which were a constant reminder of the fragility of the higher form of civilization that had been achieved through the hard work of the inhabitants of the valley of the two rivers and was the perpetual envy of their neighbours. Without these walls the town could not have existed; they required constant upkeep, and the Assyrian kings took as much pride in them as in the temples and palaces. For the town walls led to the outer world, and the gates had become important assembly points: there lawsuits were heard, there the caravans stopped, there news could be gathered, there the elders met and gave advice that was listened to respectfully, for the Semitic world had a high regard for experience. This was the setting in which the Sumerian, Babylonian and Assyrian peoples lived, and it remained essentially unchanged for almost four millenia.

This quasi-immutability of the daily setting that archaeology has revealed can be partially explained by the character of the country, by the climate, and by the basic material indispensable to the life of the ancient Orient: without clay – and despite its disadvantages as a medium for monumental architecture – few vestiges of daily life would have survived, for fired clay, even if broken, is indestructible. It was used at first to fashion various vessels, large jars for transporting or storing goods, in thick or tapering shapes according to their function, sometimes decorated with incisions but rarely coloured. Excavators have found large numbers of bowls, cups, plates, goblets, flasks that were sometimes drawn out into the shape of a bottle, cake or cheese moulds with geometric or animal designs, strainers, lids, stands for various recipients, oil lamps, etc. Clay was also used in the furnishing of private or princely houses: for paving, which was sometimes very well finished; for canalization to carry water or wastes; for all kinds of hygienic appliances including baths; and even for open-work shutters to filter the glaring light from the few windows. Nothing could replace this readily and abundantly available raw material; it enabled the modeller to express his genius as is shown by the friezes, plaques, figurines, votive carts and boats found in abundance in both secular and religious buildings. In addition, no doubt after other materials had been tried, clay became the normal vehicle of thought and its transmission; we are dealing with a "clay civilization" and no other deserves this name so well; it testifies to an outstanding capacity for adapting to an environment.

Metal – the technique of which had been perfected, and its use spread by the Sumerians – never was and never could be in such common use, despite the imposing number of objects found during excavations, such as tools (pins, hooks, fish-hooks, axes, adzes), weapons (lances, arrow-heads, daggers) and works of art (statuettes, bas-reliefs, masks). Its foreign origin and the extensive processing it required made it a costly, indeed a luxury, product.

We have been able to recapture not only the background but also the activities of the Mesopotamians, thanks mainly to their works of art. Sometimes these depict quite humble scenes – such as the work in a dairy attached to a cattle-shed where butter and cheese were made (Tell Obeid frieze, first half of the third millenium), or a peasant riding an ox and beating it with a stick (plaque of the beginning of the second millenium) – or solemn scenes, like the presentation of a prince to a god (stele of Gudea, end of the third millenium) or a prince laying the first brick of a building (stele of Ur-Nanshe, first half of the third millenium). There are various scenes depicting kings and deities, whose religious significance – at least until the Assyrian period – cannot be in any doubt.

We can see King Assurbanipal passing in his ceremonial carriage or hunting lions (bas-reliefs of Nineveh, 7th century), and witness the many victorious campaigns that the Mesopotamian sovereigns commemorated in visual records, from the stele of the vultures (first half of the third millenium) to the Assyrian bas-reliefs and the bronze plaques of Balawat (first half of the first millenium), by way of the stele of Naram-Sin (second half of the third millenium) and the standard of Ur (first half of the third millenium). We can enter the sometimes strange world of gods and heroes in the many scenes showing the presentation of a king to a god (steles and cylinders) or the exploits of Gilgamesh, especially his fights with lions.

Every object, every building, of the Middle East thus helps to reveal the state of knowledge, the material setting and the artistic environment in which Mesopotamian thought developed.

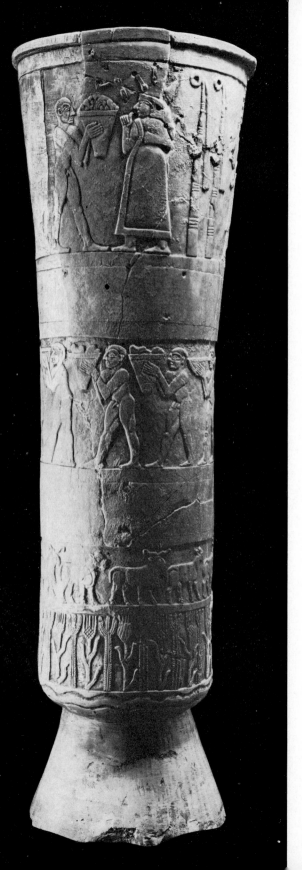

94

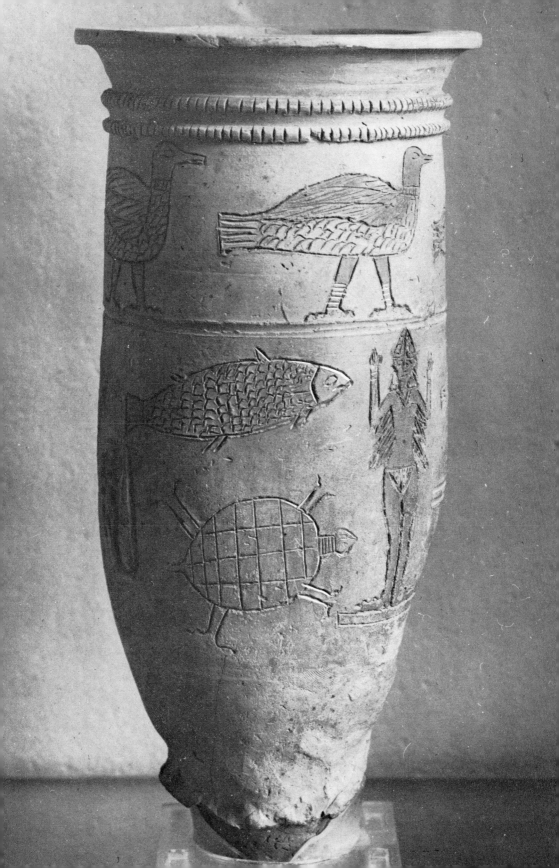

105

104

106

107

108

THE MANIFESTATION OF THOUGHT

VI

Historical research into collective attitudes and ways of thought is a recent development; despite the difficulties involved, archaeology has made some contribution to this work.

While we cannot paint a complete picture of Mesopotamian thought, some of its manifestations can be defined, despite two major obstacles. First of all–and many scholars are only too well aware of this – we are still at the stage of assembling the necessary documentation; tomorrow's excavations may well throw doubt on today's conclusions; synthesis is possible only if we regard it as a step towards a more thorough understanding. The second obstacle, which is only another aspect of the first, is that the steady progress of research and the resulting increase of knowledge show clearly that the archaic periods – for which documentation is either scanty or difficult to interpret – appear to have played a fundamental role. In the formation of artistic concepts and in the elaboration of thought, the pre-Sargon period evolved principles that dominated all later developments; to these were added the contributions and ways of thought of other populations that were integrated rather later in the Mesopotamian world. The Sumerians were the true forerunners and we cannot understand later phases, whatever their individual expression. if we do not first know Sumer. The great invention of writing belonged solely to the Sumerian civilization and this gave it a unique place in the ancient world. The Sumerians were well aware of this: they loved exploiting every possibility offered by the new technique, and this greatly influenced the subsequent development of thought and science. One example of the important part played by writing is found in the "doctrine of the name" which implied a transference of reality (and the knowledge of reality) to the name (and thus to the knowledge of names). If the name alone confers on an object its reality, that is, an individual existence, and enables it to stand out from the anonymity of matter, if knowing the word imparts power over things, then the ability to write that name, to carve it into the solid stone of statues, confers a sort of immutability on it. The written word thus took on an increasing value after an initial stage in which writing was regarded only as an economic instrument and not as a means of transmitting or preserving scientific thought, intellectual speculation or religious beliefs. In fact, religion was the last to utilize this discovery, but once it had adopted it, it made it into an essential element of sacred knowledge – an esoteric kind of knowledge based on the use of ancient written texts, that is on Sumerian which remained the language of religion for two millenia; the holders of this knowledge were especially addicted to a somewhat enigmatic form of word play, involving etymology and associations of sounds and words, which produced tales known even to the Greeks, such as that of Gyges.[21]

Once writing had taken root in the life of the Sumerians, they could not do without it; moreover, it led to the establishment of a social category with new status, qualifications and powers. The long apprenticeship needed to acquire the skill of writing with its magic associations made the scribes an important and respected class in the Sumerian, Akkadian and Assyro-Babylonian societies. A very necessary simplification finally led to the retention of only a third of the original two thousand pictographs of the script; even so, its study was a lengthy business and, far from limiting its aim to mere technical accomplishment, opened the gates of science. It meant a long attendance at the school of the temple or palace, and this alone conferred prestige. Moreover, as scribes were few in number and a large section of the population needed their services, they became indispensable intermediaries; there were various grades in this social group, from the public scribe who sat at the city gate where business was transacted, to the royal scribes and priests who alone had the right to read certain sacred texts; the priest-scribe became an intermediary between men and the gods. Placed thus at the centre of affairs, the scribe could use his social standing, his profession and his knowledge to acquire remarkable power. Although the kings themselves rarely had time to undergo the long apprenticeship, this explains why some members of the royal family became notable scribes. The study of the symbols used yields fairly accurate information on the nature of various objects at the moment when they were classified and simplified, and still more on the manner in which the Sumerians regarded these objects, i.e., the world, and on their powers of abstraction when each ideogram was formed. Thus, the ideogram for a temple consists of a trapeze (a terrace) surmounted by a square (the shrine); this proves that at the time of its formation the temple was seen only as being perched on a high terrace and that it was the façade (in view of the square shape) and not the side that was impressed on the minds of those wishing to represent it. The representation of the roof as flat shows that the people who constructed the type of building found by archaeologists at Uruk, for instance, were the same as those who invented the script. Finally, the ideogram suggests that the first Sumerians were capable of a measure of abstraction and of distinguishing the characteristic lines of the object to be represented from a rather complex whole. The evolution of each sign, which throws light on the manual skill of the scribes and on the development of techniques,[22] has been the subject of numerous studies; it can be followed to the moment when, as a result of changes and improvements – sometimes structural modifications[23] – the scribes themselves could not recognize the original sign.

All through their history, the Mesopotamians were greatly attached to religion, and the archaeologist's preference for excavating zones of worship is not solely due to the certainty of reaping a rich harvest of information. The zones devoted to the deities occupied a place of importance in the city and sometimes remained on the same sites for more than three millenia. However, a slow evolution led to a change in the basic attitude: the Sumerians had forged a theocratic State whose centre was the temple, which was sometimes oval in form and thus symbolic, since all life converged on it; each temple was the centre of a universe whose existence depended on the goodwill of the god; the whole life of the city, at Uruk as at Tell Obeid or at Khafaja, was organized in terms of religious belief. In the preceding chapter we followed the architectural evolution of the Mesopotamian temples; here we must add that it corresponded to a change in mentality. In fact, the house temple which succeeded the temple on a terrace – often a very small building whose function is not always clear in the absence of ritual objects – is characteristic of a tendency peculiar to the Semitic peoples who regarded religion as an individual rather than a collective matter; this, no doubt, explains the relative decline in the role of the temple. Whatever religion may have lost in glitter and solemnity with the development of house temples was amply made up for by the ziggurats; their shape varied considerably as is shown by the parts preserved of those of Ur, Aqarquf, Tchoga-Zembil and Khorsabad, but they were never lacking in grandeur and power; tapering from a massive base towards the sky, they seem to express a will to force a contact with the deity, to remain in touch, that had its roots in the beginning of time when royalty "descended from heaven". They do not reveal their exact purpose, but whether they were built for the celebration of the rites of the hierogamy[24] or rather, as A. Parrot thinks, as a sort of ladder inviting the deity to come down among men, they always symbolized a desire for liaison with the world of the gods. Thus the architectural discoveries of the archaeologists provide us with clues to the spiritual attitudes of the peoples of Mesopotamia.

Judging from the texts and the number and wealth of the temples, the Mesopotamians appear to have been a very religious people. It is difficult to know, however, whether routine or a deep faith was predominant in these outer expressions of a form of worship in which the people took part, as is shown by the numerous votive offerings. On the other hand, mythology shows that they were preoccupied by the great problems of life and death. But their idea of the Beyond and the after-life led there, as related by Enkidu to Gilgamesh,[25] was hardly encouraging; and since there was no hope of happiness in a future life and the life of this world was constantly endangered by floods, drought and invasions, the main boon asked of the gods was an assurance of life, the continuance of earthly existence. In their prayers to the gods, the kings of the second and first millenia asked for a long, safe reign; the great fear of death moved the Assyrian sovereigns to fill their palaces with protective animals and genii bearing the signs of life as if their presence in large numbers could ensure effective protection. This fear is a sign of the vast gulf that separated gods and men; for immortality, the attribute of the gods, could never be given to man. Uta-Napishtim alone, the tenth king before the Flood and the Babylonian equivalent of Noah, found grace with the gods and was rewarded for his piety and justice with the gift of eternal life while the rest of mankind perished in the famous cataclysm. There were heroes who attempted to appropriate or obtain immortality, but always in vain. Eternal life was reserved to the gods, and the myths reminded mortals of this fact when they were too presumptuous; nevertheless, with unexpected daring Naram-Sin is represented on a stele as having horns, the attribute of the gods, and Dingi and Bur-Sin at Ur and Ur-Ningirsu and Ugme at Lagash built hypogea that were also intended as places of worship, while the pious Gudea himself was called "the Divine" after his death; but this was only a somewhat baffling interlude in a long tradition of humility, and it disappeared with the fall of Sumer.

The Sumerian framework of this religion survived relatively unchanged until the beginning of the Christian era; this fact makes it very difficult to study, for its substance was certainly modified by the beliefs of the Semitic peoples, which did not, however, make it any more hopeful. This shortcoming was responsible for its inability to resist the spread of the Christian gospel. Although it was a religion without hope or certitude, it could nevertheless on occasion express a joy derived from its deep awareness of its origin in nature: the feast of the hierogamy, the sacred marriage of the king and the priestess which not only symbolized the union of Dumuzi and Innina but also brought it about, was celebrated amidst great popular merrymaking and closed with a ritual banquet at which the people, the king and the priestess were assembled and mimes were performed. Except on certain great occasions, the temple was not generally a meeting place of the masses; the courtyard might be used for processions, but large assemblies were not normally allowed there, and it was usually individuals or small groups who went to offer sacrifices or libations. The statue of the god, placed in the darkest part of the *cella*, the scent of aromatic plants, sacred music produced by harps, lyres, dulcimers and cymbals, the tubs and cisterns into which flowed the libations of the lustral waters, the dancing light of the oil lamps and torches reflected in the eyes of the votive statues placed on benches round the room – all these created an atmosphere of magic, a borderland between the human and divine worlds. Nowhere else would the devotee feel so close to destiny, his own destiny, the will of the gods towards him, a concept which the Babylonian felt so deeply that his only weapon against fate was the performance of religious rites; he had to influence the decisions of the gods, and what better way to do so than by performing certain acts in the hope that they would, by analogy, raise an echo in the world of the gods and move them to bend the course of destiny in a more favourable direction?

To the Mesopotamians this analogical method was a way both of acting and of thinking; from it were derived the systems of magic and divination commonly practised, and also an esotericism which became characteristic of the Oriental world. The esoteric teaching which had its source in the temples could not, by its very nature, come down to us, but here and there we can detect its existence. The sense of mystery, of the divine and the secret, was further strengthened by the retention of Sumerian as the religious and sacred language; Sumerian was the source of all culture for the Assyro-Babylonians, and its use was also a tribute to a people to whom they owed a great deal of their science. For the Mesopotamians did not content themselves with the occult, propitiatory and divining sciences, they also studied astronomy and particularly mathematics, a subject that had previously been unexplored. Thanks to the tablets, philologists and mathematicians have been able to ascertain that they knew the rudimentary operations, including division carried out by means of tables that show an advanced knowledge of fractions and the concept of squares and square roots; even quadratic equations were in common use. But we find only concrete cases, examples of problems, never any theory; this was undoubtedly transmitted orally in an esoteric form. Such knowledge was held not only by the "Chaldeans" of the later period of whom Ptolemy spoke, and its beginnings no doubt go back to the most distant antiquity. However, the Mesopotamians were not able to raise it to a coherent system independent of religious thought, and that was why – unlike the Greeks – they did not attain the universal.

The realm of art, more than any other, reflects the sense of the holy and the religious motivation in all the acts of the ancients. The mainspring of artistic creation was not aestheticism nor the search for formal beauty, but efficiency; how else can we explain the fact that so many works were not exposed to the eyes of connoisseurs but hidden in foundations of buildings or, like the statues, placed out of sight on benches in dark rooms? But their presence in these secluded places illustrates the creative role assigned to them, for they were placed there to perpetuate an attitude of prayer, offering or thanksgiving; statuary, painting and sometimes engraved gems were thus created to ensure the permanence of a pious action or an attitude intended to bring the greatest good to the person shown. In this way a work of art became a means by which man influenced the world of the gods. In the course of a long history a natural evolution led to a certain indifference to this religious purpose; while the genii in the Assyrian palaces were meant to protect the king, the more decorative bas-reliefs were surely intended to remind men of his might.

Thus, the work of art did not seek to reproduce the real but to interpret it and emphasize one or another aspect of it. In Sumerian statuary, the head is the dominant feature; on the bas-reliefs and steles (especially in the earlier periods) the prince always dominates the scene by his stature, unless he is shown in the presence of a god, this being a simple method of emphasizing hierarchical differences between the persons shown. The eyes, rendered particularly alive by the use of incrustation, had a fixedness of silent prayer which gave the faces an almost visionary intensity, especially when they were deliberately enlarged by the sculptor beyond all semblance of reality (as at Tell Asmar) to show man's dazzlement before the deity or the god's total view of the world, according to whether they are interpreted as human or as divine figures.

Although Mesopotamian art remained conventional throughout its history, it did not remain static, and there are many differences between Sumerian steles and Assyrian bas-reliefs; moreover, the rules guiding artistic production did not prevent some artists from achieving great depth. We are filled with admiration for the mask of a woman, dating from the beginning of the third millenium and found at Uruk; although it admittedly was unique for the earlier periods, it testifies to the remarkable skill, delicacy and sensibility of the sculptor. Another deservedly famous piece shows a dying lioness dragging her wounded hindquarters and roaring with rage, pain and frustration. This introduces us to a field in which Mesopotamian artists had been especially gifted from the earliest antiquity: other examples are the portrayal of a young deer grazing and the contrasting scene in which horses and gazelles flee in panic before the hunter. All these reveal a profound awareness of nature that existed side by side with religious conventions as well as abstraction and generalization (in archaic pottery and gem-engraving, for instance) and an imagination that delighted in creating a fantastic world of genii, demons and monsters (e.g., Pazuzu or Humbaba).

CONCLUSION

Archaeology is usually regarded as the daughter and handmaid of history; judging *a posteriori* from the results achieved on Mesopotamian soil, we must, however, admit that it has won its claim to recognition in its own right. While it has contributed a rich harvest of material to history, archaeology has above all made it possible to rediscover a civilization of almost four thousand years ago. Every stage of its development has been re-captured: the Neolithic, the change to an urban civilization thanks to the discovery of me-tal-working and of writing – the features that were partly responsible for the uniqueness of Sumer; the struggle between the ethnic groups of Sumerians and Semites, the fall of Sumer at the beginning of the second millenium, but the survival of its thought, though modified by the Assyro-Babylonian mind; the amazing spread of the growing civilization at the beginning of the second half of the second millenium; the formation of the great Assyrian, Babylonian and Persian empires. Every aspect – thought, background, strength and weakness – has gradually been revealed. Moreover, this astonishing resurrection has carried the origins of our Western civilization back by three millenia. The beginning of the excavations showed that the modern world had inherited a part of the Mesopotamian legacy by way of the Bible whose mythical and religious subject matter, originating in the Orient, forms a basic aspect of Western civilization. But it has also become clear that we must revi-se and redefine our views on the specific features of Greece, on the conditions in which its thought was developed, and on its originality; for while the "Greek miracle" was real, it was made possible only by the contribution of the Orient, both as regards its religious thought and its scientific discoveries. Thus the Babylonian myth of Creation, with the victory of Marduk, king of the gods and organizer of the world, over Tiamat, the symbol of chaos and the Chthonian forces, is found in its essentials in the victorious struggle of Zeus against Typhon: this is not a coincidence but rather the result of the spread of Mesopotamian thought which, in the second millenium, reached the Mycenaean civiliza-tion and thus the nascent Greek world by way of the Hittites and the Phoenicians. If we think of Greece as the cradle of modern thought, it is because Greece was able to pass beyond the stage of individualism and attain the universal; but it was the Mesopotamian world that took the first steps, produced the first great civilization and bestowed its benefits on its neighbours and successors. This is the knowledge we have gained from Mesopotamian archaeology.

113

115

114

116

117

118

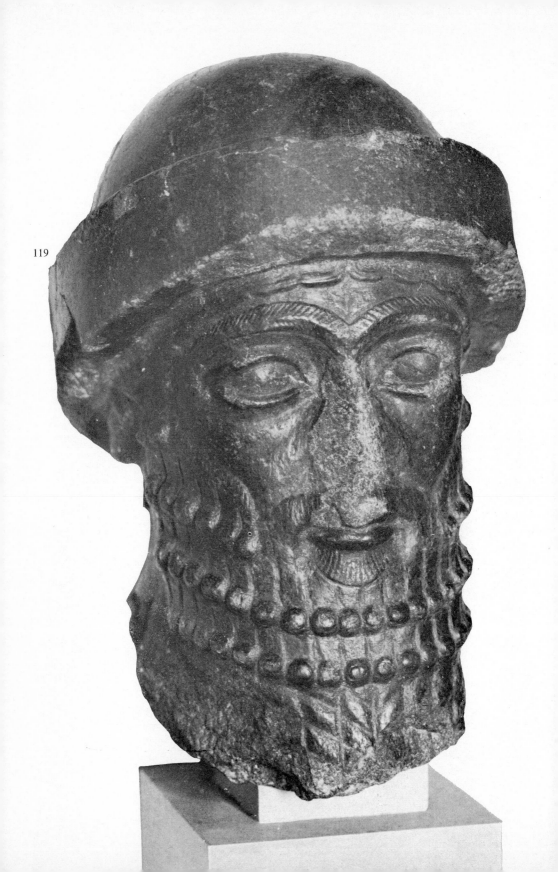

119

130 →

[1] In its strict sense, Mesopotamia means "the country between the rivers" and comprises the region between the Tigris and the Euphrates, with the regions of Khabur and Assyria in the north, the middle Euphrates and the valley of the Diyala in the centre, then Babylonia, and finally, completely to the south, the land of Sumer. The word is used only exceptionally outside these limits; we must remember that the concept of Mesopotamia is, in fact, a modern one; the Ancients were not clearly aware of the unity of the region, and the empire of Hammurabi which extended more or less over this area, was an exception. City states, kingdoms and empires succeeded one another in the region or co-existed in it without seeking to form a coherent geographical state, though trying to expand as much as opportunity permitted; the Assyrian and then the Achaemenid empires show that the strictly geographical limits are not always valid.

[2] A village just north of Tell Quyundjiq was called Niniouah during the last century.

[3] A kudurru is a stele covered with bas-reliefs and inscriptions; placed in a temple, it conferred a sacred character on property.

[4] Syllabary: a sort of list giving the phonetic and ideographic values for each symbol.

[5] Quoted in Fossey, *Manuel d'Assyriologie*, I.

[6] Quoted in Fossey, *Manuel d'Assyriologie*, I.

[7] A. Parrot, *Archéologie mésopotamienne* I.

[8] Title conferred in the Sumerian civilization on one having civil and religious authority in the city.

[9] A. Parrot in A. Varagnac: *L'Homme avant l'histoire*, p. 191, A. Colin, 1959.

[10] The work of this expedition was not confined to the Diyala but has spread throughout the Middle East over the last thirty years.

[11] Some sites are not being worked regularly: thus S. Williams on two occasions – in 1956 and 1960 – excavated Tell Rifa'at, the capital of the Aramaean state of Big Agusi, and in 1960 D. Stonach investigated the prehistoric site of Ras Al Amiya, not far from Kish.

[12] J. R. Kupper, *Les Nomades en Mésopotamie au temps des rois de Mari*, Paris. Les Belles Lettres, 1957.

[13] J. Deshayes: *Les outils de l'âge du bronze de l'Indus au Danube (IV au IIe millénaire)*. Paris, 1960. *Comptes rendus de la deuxième Rencontre Assyriologique Internationale*. Paris, 1951.
R. I. Forbes: *Metallurgy in Antiquity*, 1950.

[14] H. Limet: *Le Travail du métal à Sumer au temps de la IIIe dynastie d'Ur*. Paris. Les Belles Lettres, 1960.

[15] For instance, J. Bottero: *La Religion babylonienne*. P. U. F., Paris, 1952.

[16] S. Lloyd recounts that, when he was excavating at Hassuna during the last war, the wind one night was so strong that it blew all the kitchen material a distance of more than a quarter of a mile.

[17] Fossey: *Manuel d'Assyriologie*. Preface: "... some people seem to have regarded archaeology only as an auxiliary science to Biblical studies, or at least have studied the Assyrian texts with the constant and evident concern to find in them the justification for their preconceived ideas on the historical value of Biblical accounts or, in the opposite camp, on the extent to which Isreael borrowed from the Babylonian civilization ... I hardly need to say here how much I disapprove of this unscientific approach."

[18] Cf. A. Parrot: *Babylone et l'Ancien Testament*.

[19] However, we must give credit to Iraq which has undertaken preservation and restoration work, especially at Hatra, at Ur (ziggurat) and at Babylon (processional way) in order to prevent the loss of all the vestiges of its past.

[20] Lions were feared but also sought-after animals: a letter found in the palace at Mari shows the perplexity of one of the king's servants who did not know what to do, in his master's absence, with a captured lion that refused to eat.

[21] G. Dossin in *Le Sumérien, langue savante et religieuse* points out the connexion between this legend as told by Piato (for which, however, we have no Oriental version) and a certain number of Sumerograms GUGU, GIG(I), GI(G). the first of which is the origin of the name of the king of Lydia, while the others contain all the basic features of the tale: the sheep, the hole or cave, the ring, return and invisible.

[22] Originally the symbols were drawn from top to bottom, starting at the upper right-hand corner, then the ideograms seem to have made a quarter-turn to the left so that they look as if they were lying down. This change was probably due to the fact that the tablets were held in the left hand and that the signs were engraved in the softened clay from the right with the help of a calamus; in this position it was easier to move the hand from left to right rather than from top to bottom, without changing anything in the general layout. The habit of writing the signs in this manner soon led to the tablets being held in the same position when it was being read; however, on some inscriptions carved on stone buildings the vertical writing continued.

[23] The use of the calamus which imprinted a part of the sign in a straight line, did away with the curves of the original drawings and led to the "nail" shape, the main element of the symbol.

[24] A rite ensuring fertility by a mystical marriage; see page 176.

[25] At the end of the epic, Gilgamesh succeeded in communicating with the spirit of Enkidu who described to him (from the depth of hell) an underground world plunged in darkness, where there was no rest, no physical or spiritual satisfaction, only nakedness, worms, and dust – a world that could only make the living "weep".

A SHORT BIBLIOGRAPHY

A. Aymard and J. Auboyer: *L'Orient et la Grèce antique*, vol. I. Histoire générale des Civilisations. Paris 1957.

G. Contenau: *La civilisation d'Assur et de Babylone*. Payot. Paris 1951.

G. Contenau: *L'Epopée de Gilgamesh, poème babylonien*. L'artisan du livre. Paris 1939.

G. Contenau: *Manuel d'archéologie orientale*. Picard. 4 vols. Paris 1927–1947.

E. Dhorme: *Les religions de Babylone et d'Assyrie*. Coll. Mana. P.U.F. 1949.

H. Fischer: *L'aube de la civilisation en Egypte et en Mésopotamie*. Payot. Paris 1964.

Ch. Fossey: *Manuel d'assyriologie*. Paris 1964.

H. Frankfort: *The art and architecture of the ancient Orient*. The Pelican History of Art. Penguin Books. 1954.

G. Goossens: *Asie occidentale ancienne*. In Histoire universelle: Encyclopédie de la Pléiade, tome I, Des origines à l'Islam. N.R.F. 1956.

R. Labat: *La Mésopotamie* in *La science antique et médiévale*. Vol. I of Histoire générale des Sciences. Paris 1957.

S. Lloyd: *Mounds of the Near East*. Edinburgh University Press 1963.

S. Moscatti: *L'Orient avant les Grecs*. P.U.F. Paris 1963.

S. Pallis: *The Antiquity of Iraq*. Ejnar Munksgaard. Copenhagen 1956.

A. Parrot: *Archéologie mésopotamienne*. Albin Michel. Vol. I: Les étapes. 1946. Vol. II: Techniques et problèmes. 1953.

A. Parrot: *Sumer*. Coll. L'univers des formes. N.R.F. 1960.

A. Parrot: *Assur*. Coll. L'univers des formes. N.R.F. 1961.

A. Parrot: *Babylone et l'Ancien Testament*. Cahier d'archéologie biblique 8. Delachaux et Niestlé. 1956.

A. Parrot: *Ziqqurats et tour de Babel*. A. Michel. Paris 1949.

M. Rutten: *La Science des Chaldéens*. Que sais-je? P.U.F. 1960.

M. Rutten: *Les arts du Moyen-Orient ancien*. Coll. Les neuf Muses. P.U.F. 1962.

H. Schmökel: *Sumer et la civilisation sumérienne*. Payot. Paris 1964.

H. Schmökel: *Le monde d'Ur, Assur et Babylone*. Editions Corrêa Buchet-Chastel. Paris 1957.

Ch. Virolleaud: *Légendes de Babylone et de Canaan*. Coll. L'Orient ancien illustré 1. A. Maisonneuve. Paris 1949.

Sir Charles Leonard Woolley: *Mesopotamia and the Middle East*. Methuen, London, 1961.

Sir Charles Leonard Woolley: *Excavations at Ur*. Ernest Benn. London, 1963.

LIST OF ILLUSTRATIONS

21 *The demon Pazuzu with outspread wings. Bronze. Height: approx. 3 inches. Neo-Babylonian period. Louvre.*

22 *Game from Ur. Inlay of shell, lapis lazuli, pink stone, bitumen, etc. 1st half of the 3rd millennium. Length: 10.6 inches. British Museum.*

23 *Bronze lion guarding the temple of Dagan at Mari. Beginning of the 2nd millennium. Length: 27.5 inches. Louvre.*

24 *Upright ram and bush. Gold, lapis lazuli, shell, silver, etc. Ur. 1st half of the 3rd millennium. Height: 20 inches. British Museum.*

25 *Painted pottery in the style of El Obeid. Ur. 4th–3rd millennium. Height: 2.2 inches. Diameter: 8.7 inches. British Museum.*

26 *Monumental bronze lance dedicated by a king of Kish. Lagash. 1st half of the 3rd millennium. Length: 31 inches. Width: 5 inches. Louvre.*

27a *Bust of Sa-ud, the grandson of Lugalkisalsi, King of Uruk. Lagash(?). Middle of the 3rd millennium. Limestone. Height: 11 inches. Louvre.*

27b *Lupad, a high official of Umma. Middle of the 3rd millennium. Height: 16 inches. Louvre.*

27c *King Iku-Shamagan of Mari. 1st half of the 3rd millennium. Plaster. Height: 36.2 inches. Damascus Museum.*

27d *Idi-Narum, a miller. Pink breccia. Mari. 1st half of the 3rd millennium. Height: 8 inches. Aleppo Museum.*

28 *Woman with scarf. Lagash. 22nd century. Steatite. Height: 3.9 inches. Louvre.*

29 *Pottery decorated with human figures. Diyala. 4th–3rd millennium. Bagdad Museum.*

30 *Detail from a mural painting in the palace of Til-Barsip. 8th century B.C. Height: 13.8 inches. Aleppo Museum.*

31 *Head of a man. Terracotta. Mari. Louvre.*

32 *Bronze head, probably of King Sargon of Akkad. Nineveh, Akkadian art. 2nd half of the 3rd millennium. Height: 11.8 inches. Bagdad Museum.*

33 *Head of a deity. Terracotta. Lagash, Akkadian art. 2nd half of the 3rd millennium. Height: 3.9 inches. Louvre.*

34 *"Turbaned" head of Gudea, the spiritual and temporal ruler of Lagash. 22nd century. Diorite. Height: 9.4 inches. Louvre.*

35 *Woman's head. Marble. Uruk. 1st half of the 3rd millennium. Height: 8 inches. Bagdad Museum.*

36 *Woman's head. Limestone. Mari style. Adab? 3rd millennium. Height: approx: 2 inches. Louvre.*

37 *Woman's head. Calcareous sandstone with eyes inlaid in shell and lapis lazuli. Khafa-jah. Middle of the 3rd millennium. Height: 2.7 inches. Nelson Gallery of Art, Kansas City (Missouri).*

38 *Woman's head. Plaster. Assur, Akkadian art. 2nd half of the 3rd millennium. Height: 2.7 inches. Staatliche Museen, Berlin.*

39 *Statue of a goddess with a vase. White stone. Mari. 18th century B.C. Height: 58.7 inches. Aleppo Museum.*

40 *Ivory mirror handle. From Birs Nimrud, ancient Borsippa. 1st millennium. Height: approx. 4.7 inches. British Museum.*

41 *Alabaster statuette of Ishtar. Babylon. 1st millennium. Height: approx. 9.5 inches. Louvre.*

42 *Ring. Enamelled gold with lapis lazuli and cornelian. Lagash. Approx. middle of the 3rd millennium. Height: 0.5 inch. Diameter: 1 inch. Louvre.*

43 *Gold and cornelian jewels from Mari. Beginning of the 2nd millennium. Louvre.*

44 *Terracotta chariot. Babylon. 1st half of the 2nd millennium. Height: approx. 8 inches. Louvre.*

45 *Votive chariot. Copper. Tell Agrab. 1st half of the 3rd millennium. Height: 2.7 inches. Bagdad Museum.*

46 *Bas-relief of servants carrying the king's chariot. Dur-Sharrukin. 8th century B.C. Height: 113 inches. Width: 96 inches. Louvre.*

47 *Small silver boat from the tomb of "king" Abargi at Ur. 1st half of the 3rd millennium. Bagdad Museum.*

48 *Lapis lazuli cylinder of a sacred boat. Uruk. 1st half of the 3rd millennium. Height: 1.7 inches. Staatliche Museen, Berlin.*

49 *Bas-relief, gypseous alabaster, showing the transport of wood on the Phoenician coast. Dur-Sharrukin. 8th century B.C. Length of boat: 31 inches. Height of boat: 17 inches. Total height: 115 inches. Louvre.*

50 *Gudea, "the architect with the plan". Lagash. 22nd century. Diorite. Height: 36.6 inches. Louvre.*

51 *Libation goblet of Gudea, the spiritual and temporal ruler of Lagash. 22nd century. Steatite. Height: 9 inches. Louvre.*

52 *Cylinders of Gudea. 22nd century. Terracotta. Height: 23 and 21 inches. Louvre.*

53 *Small seated Gudea. Diorite. Lagash. 22nd century. Height: 17.7 inches. Louvre.*

54 *Imdugud, a lion-headed eagle, joining two stags. Copper. Temple of Ninhursag at El Obeid. 1st half of the 3rd millennium. Height: 42 inches. Length: 92.5 inches. British Museum.*

55   *Chequer-board from the "royal" tombs at Ur. Carved shell, lapis lazuli, limestone. Middle of the 3rd millennium. University Museum, Philadelphia.*

56   *Plaque with two facing ibexes. Bagdad Museum.*

57   *The sun-god, Shamash, holding the emblems of power; inscription of Nabu-Apal-Iddin. Sippar. 9th century B.C. Stone. Width: 7.1 inches. British Museum.*

58   *Stone stele of Assurbanipal. Babylon. 7th century B.C. Height: 15.2 inches. British Museum.*

59   *Ivory panel of a young man with a lotus. Kalakh. Beginning of the 1st millennium B.C. Height: 3.8 inches. British Museum.*

60   *Limestone stele of Sham Shi-Adad V of Assur. Kalakh. 9th century B.C. Height: 115 inches. British Museum.*

61   *Alabaster statue of Assurnazirpal II. Kalakh. 9th century B.C. Height: 42 inches. British Museum.*

62   *Detail from the prism of Sennacherib: specimen of cuneiform writing. Assyrian. Terracotta. 1st half of the 3rd millennium. British Museum.*

63   *Clay tablet inscribed in cuneiform with an account of the exploits of Sargon of Akkad, with a map of Babylonia and Assyria surrounded by the ocean. 7th–6th century B.C., from Abu Habba, ancient Sippar. Height: approx. 4.8 inches. British Museum.*

64   *Harp from the tomb of "Queen" Sh-ubad at Ur. Mosaics, on wood, made of shell, lapis lazuli and red stones. 1st half of the 3rd millennium. Height: 42.1 inches. British Museum.*

65   *Detail of the above.*

66   *Terracotta plaque of a harpist. Eshnunna. Beginning of the 2nd millennium. Height: 5 inches. Width: 3 inches. Louvre.*

67   *Banquet scene. Perforated limestone plaque. Khafajah; the lower part, left, comes from Ur. 1st half of the 3rd millennium. Height: 11.6 inches. Bagdad Museum.*

68   *Plaster statuette of Ur-nanshe, the "great singer". Mari. 1st half of the 3rd millennium. Height: 10.2 inches. Damascus Museum.*

69   *Alabaster bas-relief, "resting under the vine". Nineveh. 7th century B.C. Height: 54 inches. Even this scene of quiet and rest has a war-like feature — so typical of that civilization – in the form of the head of the vanquished enemy hanging from a tree.*

70–71   *Details from plate 69.*

72   *Gypseous alabaster bas-relief of prisoners playing the lyre. Nineveh. 7th century B.C. Height: 30 inches. British Museum.*

73   *Ritual vase decorated with lions and bulls. Limestone. Uruk. 1st half of the 3rd millennium. Height: 8 inches. Bagdad Museum. (Copy in Berlin).*

74　Limestone slab carved in relief with scene of Assyrian horsemen pursuing an enemy Reign of Tiglath Pileser III (745–727 B.C.), from S.-W. Palace, Nimrud. Height: 46.8 inches. British Museum.

75　Ivory calf's head. 9th–8th century B.C., from Abu Habba, ancient Sippar. Height: approx. 3.2 inches. British Museum.

76　Gypseous alabaster bas-relief of Gilgamesh with a lion cub. Dur-Sharrukin. 8th century B.C. Height: 185 inches. Louvre.

77　Detail from a gypseous alabaster bas-relief of a wounded lioness. Nineveh. 7th century B.C. Height: 23.6 inches. British Museum.

78　Terracotta mould from the kitchens of the palace at Mari. 18th century B.C. Length: 11.5 inches. Height: 2.1 inches. Width: 4.7 inches. Louvre.

79　Golden cup with spout from a royal tomb, at Ur. 1st half of the 3rd millennium. Height: 4.9 inches. British Museum.

80　Ivory plaque of a young man overwhelmed by a lioness. Kalakh. 8th–7th century B.C. Height: 4.1 inches. British Museum.

81　Mace of the Uruk period. 1st half of the 3rd millennium. Height: approx. 6 inches. Bagdad Museum.

82　Stele of Naram-Sin, the grandson of Sargon of Akkad. Found at Susa. 2nd half of the 3rd millennium. Red sandstone. Height: 78.7 inches. Width: 41.3 inches. Louvre.

83　Detail from the above.

84　Fragment of the Stele of the Vultures: Eannatum at the head of his troops. Lagash. Middle of the 3rd millennium. Limestone. Total height: 74 inches. Louvre.

85　Terracotta figurine, "the warrior with the adze". Lagash. 21st century. Height: 7.5 inches. Bagdad Museum.

86　Alabaster bas-relief of Assurbanipal on his chariot. Nineveh. 7th century B.C. Height: 31 inches. Louvre.

87　Ivory horse nasal with a naked goddess. Kalakh. 8th century B.C. Height: 6.3 inches. British Museum.

88　Details from an alabaster bas-relief of prisoners-of-war. Nineveh. 7th century B.C. Total height: 47 inches. Height of a prisoner: 11 inches. Louvre.

89　Bronze facing of door illustrating the campaign of Salmanasar III in northern Phoenicia, the attack on Dabigu. The lower strip shows a scene of impaled prisoners. Imgur-Bel. 9th century B.C. Height: approx. 11 inches. British Museum.

90　Bronze facing of door illustrating the campaign of Salmanasar III in Phoenicia. The. tribute of Tyre and, in the lower strip, a procession of chariots. Imgur-Bel. 9th century B.C. Height: approx. 11 inches. British Museum.

91　Bas-relief of a besieged fortress. Kalakh. 8th century B.C. Height: 38 inches. Width: 29 inches. Louvre.

92 *Bronze facing of door illustrating the campaign of Salmanasar III in Armenia. In the lower strip, procession of captives. Imgur-Bel. 9th century B.C. Height: approx. 11 inches. British Museum.*

93 *Seal of pink agate cylinder showing a battle between a lion and a winged horse. Assyrian art. 1st half of the 1st millennium. Height: 1.5 inches. British Museum.*

94 *Alabaster libation vessel decorated with ritual scenes. Uruk. 4th–3rd millennium. Height: 41.3 inches. Bagdad Museum.*

95 *Terracotta vase. Larsa, style of Susa. Beginning of the 2nd millennium. Height: 5 inches. Louvre.*

96 *Terracotta libation vessel with incised decoration of a winged goddess and animals. Larsa. Beginning of the 2nd millennium. Height: 10.6 inches. Louvre.*

97 *Two ibexes. Fragment of a hunting scene. Bronze. 1st millennium. Height: 5 inches. Louvre.*

98 *Seal of cylinder with a stag in front of a tree. Grey chalcedony. Assyrian style. Beginning of the 1st millennium. Height: 1.1 inches. Bibliothèque Nationale, Paris.*

99 *Detail from the seal of the cylinder of the scribe Adda, showing the sungod and the god of water. Akkadian art. 2nd half of the 3rd millennium. Green schist. Height: approx. 1.5 inches. British Museum.*

100 *Cornelian cylinder with gold mount. Nezab (near Aleppo). 1st half of the 1st millennium. Louvre.*

101 *Detail of the standard of Ur. Mosaic in shell, lapis lazuli, schist, pink stone, etc. held with bitumen. 1st half of the 3rd millennium. Height: 8 inches. Total length: 18.5 inches; here: 11 inches. British Museum.*

102 *The demon Pazuzu. Bronze. Assyrian style. 1st half of the 1st millennium. Height: 6 inches. Louvre.*

103 *Winged genius in front of the sacred tree. Kalakh. 9th century B.C. Gypseous alabaster. Height: 40.5 inches. Louvre.*

104 *"Frieze of the Dairy" from the temple of Ninhursag at El Obeid. Shell and limestone inlay on a background of copper-framed schist. 1st half of the 3rd millennium. Height: 8.6 inches. Length: 45.2 inches. Bagdad Museum.*

105–106 *Head of bull. Copper with eyes of shell and lapis lazuli. Khafajah. 3rd millennium. Height: approx. 6.7 inches. Bagdad Museum.*

107 *Winged bull with man's head. Dur-Sharrukin. 8th century B.C. Gypseous alabaster. Height: 165 inches. (There were bulls on both sides of the palace entrance.) Louvre.*

108 *Detail from the "scorpion-man". Basalt. Tell Halaf. Beginning of the 1st millennium. Height: 63 inches. Length: 81 inches. Aleppo Museum.*

109 *Detail from a kudurru of King Nebuchadnezzar: A "scorpion-man" drawing the bow. 2nd dynasty of Isin. 12th century B.C.. Limestone. Height: 25.4 inches. Width: 8.3 inches. British Museum.*

110   *Bronze figurine of a Babylonian demon. Louvre.*

111   *Detail from a basalt bas-relief of a hunt with bow and falcon. Dur-Sharrukin. 8th century B.C. Height: 63.8 inches. Louvre.*

112   *Zoomorphic pottery. 3rd millennium. Bagdad Museum.*

113   *Stand from Tell Agrab. Height: 8 inches. Bagdad Museum.*

114   *Limestone trough. Uruk(?). 1st half of the 3rd millennium. Length: 39 inches. British Museum.*

115   *Terracotta mould from the kitchens of the palace at Mari. 18th century B.C. Diameter: 8.9 inches. Height: 1.5 inches.*

116   *Recumbent ram. Black stone. Uruk. 1st half of the 3rd millennium. Height: 3.9 inches. Staatliche Museen, Berlin.*

117   *Code of Hammurabi, found at Susa. 18th century B.C. Black basalt. Height: 88.5 inches. Louvre.*

118   *Detail from the above.*

119   *Head of Hammurabi(?), found at Susa. 18th century B.C. Diorite. Height: 6 inches. Louvre.*

120   *Bull. Bronze plating on wood. Frieze from the temple at El Obeid. 1st half of the 3rd millennium. Height: 47 inches. British Museum.*

121   *Dragon from the gate of Ishtar at Babylon. 7th–6th century B.C. Enamelled brick. Height: 41 inches. Staatliche Museen, Berlin.*

122   *Kneeling worshipper. Bronze statuette from Larsa. Height: 8 inches. 2nd millennium. Louvre.*

123   *Vase with painted decoration in the style of Tell Halaf. 5th–4th millennium. Height: approx. 8 inches. Bagdad Museum.*

124   *Dolerite stele of Asarhaddon holding Abdimilkutti and Ushanahuru on a leash. Zenjirli. 7th century B.C. Height: 125 inches. Staatliche Museen, Berlin.*

125   *Detail from a bas-relief of preparations for a meal. Limestone. Dur-Sharrukin. 8th century B.C. Height: 118 inches. Louvre.*

126   *Terracotta plaque of a naked woman. Larsa. Beginning of the 2nd millennium. Height: 4.1 inches. Louvre.*

127   *Terracotta plaque of a woman feeding her baby. Lagash. 3rd–2nd millennium. Height: approx. 3 inches. Louvre.*

128   *Dragon's head, an attribute of the god Marduk. Neo-Babylonian art. 7th–6th century B.C. Bronze. Height: 5.9 inches. Louvre.*

129   *Votive relief of Dudu, the high priest of Lagash. Middle of the 3rd millennium. Bituminous stone. Height: 10 inches. Louvre.*

130   *Statuette of the god Abu(?) and of a goddess. Veined gypsum. Eshnunna. 1st half of the 3rd millennium. Height: 28 and 23 inches. Bagdad Museum.*

THE TEXT AND ILLUSTRATIONS
IN THIS VOLUME WERE PRINTED
ON THE PRESSES OF NAGEL
PUBLISHERS IN GENEVA.

FINISHED IN JUNE 1965.
BINDING BY NAGEL PUBLISHERS,
GENEVA.

PLATES ENGRAVED BY AMOR S.A,
GENEVA.

LEGAL DEPOSIT NO. 365

PRINTED IN SWITZERLAND